MW00576715

SCIENCE AND THE
MIRACULOUS

SCIENCE AND THE MIRACULOUS

HOW THE CHURCH INVESTIGATES THE SUPERNATURAL

MICHAEL O'NEILL
THE MIRACLE HUNTER

TAN Books
Gastonia, North Carolina

Unless otherwise noted, Scripture quotations are from the Revised Standard Version of the Bible—Second Catholic Edition (Ignatius Edition), copyright © 2006 National Council of the Churches of Christ in the United States of America. Used by permission. All rights reserved.

Excerpts from the English translation of the Catechism of the Catholic Church for use in the United States of America © 1994, United States Catholic Conference, Inc.—Libreria Editrice Vaticana. Used with permission.

Cover design by David Ferris—www.davidferrisdesign.com.
Cover images: Our Lady of Guadalupe © SandroSalomon, Background numbers, symbols, lights and elements © agsandrew, and Holy Eucharist © Immaculate, used via Shutterstock.com.
Interior images: "Basilica of Our Lady of Guadalupe", "Virgin Mary in Window, Absam, Austria" and "Sanctuary of Las Lajas, Ipiales, Colombia" used via Wikimedia Commons CC BY-SA 4.0 and CC BY-SA 3.0 licenses. Creative Commons <https://creativecommons.org/licenses/>.

Library of Congress Control Number: 2021951932
ISBN: 978-1-5051-1639-7
Kindle ISBN: 9781505116403
ePUB ISBN: 9781505116410

Published in the United States by
TAN Books
PO Box 269
Gastonia, NC 28053
www.TANBooks.com
Printed in the United States of America

Contents

Introduction: Faith and Science

To live by faith or to live by reason? To trust science or to trust religion?

Sometimes it seems that one must choose between the two. But from scientists to priests, from saints of old to professors at modern universities, from theologians to everyday folks in the pew, Catholics have always understood how to embrace truth through the lenses of both faith and science.

"We pray together, and we do science together, and we have no sense of conflict. There is no problem," Fr. Paul Mueller, a researcher and head of the Jesuit community at the Vatican Observatory, reminded me in a radio interview.[1]

Pope Leo XIII re-founded the Vatican Observatory in 1891 to study astronomy and demonstrate that a Catholic worldview encompasses both faith and science. In fact, papal-supported astronomy is a tradition dating back to the reform of the Gregorian calendar in the 1500s. Today, it is run by the Jesuits. These priest-scientists live and work at the observatory, carrying out both their priestly duties and research roles.

For Father Mueller, faith and science are two paths to the truth, each shedding light on the Christian life in their own ways.

"Some of the most important things in our lives we believe not because science says so. Science can't say so. It's outside the realm of science to say whether or not your wife or your husband loves you. Science doesn't talk about the ultimate questions that are most important to us in life, questions of love, the good, the true, and the beautiful. You can get a good handle on some of the truth from science, but not all of it."[2]

Answers to the heart's deepest, most profound questions, such as the meaning of life, come from faith.

But the question, "Why are we here?" is also closely related to the question, "How did we get here?" Unfortunately, in today's culture, the study of creation only seems to further alienate science and religion from each other. But not among Catholic scientists.

Dr. Michael Dennin, professor of physics and astronomy at UC Irvine, spoke to me on the radio about this focus of the debate. "The common thing you hear in the press and in the public debate is always about creation and evolution. It really comes down to recognizing that most of the people who are having that debate are simply debating their assumptions. And neither of those groups has what I consider the traditional classic and orthodox Catholic view, which is: the world is more than just a physical reality that obeys physical laws. There is God; there is a reality that transcends physical reality."[3]

In sum, reason and science delve into the physical laws of reality, while faith and religion explore transcendental realities.

When I interviewed Dr. Gerard Verschuuren, a biologist and philosopher who has worked at several European and American universities, he reiterated how the discoveries of science regarding the physical realities of the earth's existence are not incompatible with the beliefs of the Catholic faith.

Dr. Verschuuren addresses the question of the age of the universe, for example, which scientists usually calculate to be 4.5 billion years, including a few billion to form the earth. It's not a figure that necessarily coincides with the biblical creation stories.

"The book of Genesis is not a science book. It has a much better message than science."

According to Dr. Verschuuren, the science of the physical laws of the earth's existence and the message of the Bible both coincide in one fact: the world as we know it is a miracle, a direct act of God. "This planet Earth has become our home," he said. "That is definitely a miracle."

The universe has been characterized by some scientists as being "finely-tuned," which suggests that the occurrence of life in the universe is entirely improbable and very sensitive to the values of certain fundamental physical constants. If the values of any of the certain free parameters had differed only slightly from those observed, the formation and development of the universe would have proceeded very differently, and life as it is we know it may not have been possible.

The earth itself is unique in many ways that allow it to be hospitable to life. The shape of its orbit, gases from volcanic activity, the luminosity of the sun, the density of the atmosphere, a magnetic field deflecting the rays of the sun, and good balance of land and water due to plate tectonics are all essential for life on our planet.[4] Even as a scientist, Dr. Verschuuren finds it easier to attribute the existence of the world to the intelligent, loving act of a Creator than to the probability of large numbers, the currently popular scientific explanation for the world's existence.

For scientists of faith, their belief in a loving Creator motivates them to understand the world God created. Science and faith can be deeply linked, as Fr. John Kartje discussed with me during an interview. Father Kartje is an astrophysicist and president and rector of the University of Saint Mary of the Lake. "For the person of faith, for the believer, the world around you is the fruit of the intersection of that creating God and the manifestation of his love. And so, of course, it makes perfect sense to say that my faith really should only be deepened as it is further informed by my study and learning of the world. I mean, all you have to do is read one page of the *Summa* to see how fascinated Saint Thomas was with just the actual perceived world that surrounded him."[5]

All these learned individuals assert the same thing: faith and science are not in conflict. They are complimentary. The book that follows will prove this by examining a series of inexplicable phenomena that have puzzled those who have studied them and deepened the faith of those who believe in them. Let us embark now on a parade through history as we explore the science behind the many miraculous events that have occurred in the life of the Church, showing us that there is a world beyond the reach of our senses, one that waits for us after our death and yet also whispers to us now through signs and wonders as we traverse this valley of tears.

A Comment on the Miraculous
Claims Found in this Text

This book runs through several millennia worth of miraculous claims from all over the world. Some are approved by the Church, some are still open for examination, and others have not been approved. The point of this work is not to comment on whether or not these cases are all true or take a stance one way or the other. Rather, the goal of this work is to examine the scientific methods we can use, and those that have been used, to better understand these events and, hopefully, bring merit to authentic cases of the miraculous by exposing fraud or by offering a natural (if not unusual and rare) explanation. The author and publisher ask that this be kept in mind as we move through these pages.

The History of the Catholic Church and Science

A Church in Support of Science

To the average person, both Catholic and non-Catholic alike, the Church may be labeled as being squarely opposed to science. No further evidence seems to be needed outside of citing the Galileo affair, the oft debated and misunderstood reaction of the Catholic Church to the astronomer's support of heliocentrism, the scientific model which states that the earth and other planets revolve around the sun at the center of the solar system.

Yet the words of modern popes paint a different picture of the Church's official view of science. In an address to the Pontifical Academy of Sciences in 2014, Pope Francis dispelled the notion that faith would have a problem with science with a reminder that everything we find in science points to a Creator: "The Big Bang theory, which is proposed today as the origin of the world, does not contradict the intervention of a divine creator but depends on it. Evolution in nature does not conflict with the notion of Creation, because evolution presupposes the creation of beings who evolve."[6]

His predecessor, Pope Benedict XVI, extolled the unsurpassed value of science: "Art along with science is the highest gift God has given [man]."[7]

Still more, in a 1988 letter to the director of the Vatican Observatory, Pope St. John Paul II even went as far as to indicate the complementarity of science and religion: "Science can purify religion from error and superstition; religion can purify science from idolatry and false absolutes."[8]

The *Catechism of the Catholic Church* likewise affirms the absence of conflict between faith and reason: "Though faith is above reason, there can never be any real discrepancy between faith and reason. Since the same God who reveals mysteries and infuses faith has bestowed the light of reason on the human mind, God cannot deny himself, nor can truth ever contradict truth."[9]

In many ways, science owes its advancement to the structures put in place through the growth of Christianity. The Catholic Church has been a patron of science and responsible for the foundation and funding of schools, universities, and hospitals. The development of Catholic nursing and hospital systems reflecting the central Christian virtue of charity has resulted in the establishment and persistence of the Church as the single largest private provider of medical care and research facilities in the world.[10]

In the earliest centuries of the Church and beyond, western Europe's scholarship is tied to the clergy and religious in monasteries and convents with an eventual focus on the natural sciences, mathematics, and astronomy. The Middle Ages then saw the foundation of Europe's first universities by the Catholic Church. Fr. Stanley L. Jaki, famed physicist and author of *The Relevance of Physics* (1966) and *Science and Creation* (1974), argued that "the scientific enterprise did not become viable and self-sustaining until its incarnation in Christian medieval Europe, and that the advancement of science was indebted to the Christian understanding of creation."[11] These universities produced both the scholars and the scientific method.

Alvin J. Schmidt, author of *How Christianity Changed the World*, suggests that the inductive empirical method of acquiring knowledge—the essential building block of all modern science whereby rational processes are used to study and investigate the world—was the result of belief in a single, rational, personal deity, who as the creator of the natural world was in fact distinct from the natural world, thus opening the doors for its rational study and exploration. This thereby overcame the prevailing and longstanding Aristotelian mindset that for 1,500 years had established the unchallenged notion that all knowledge came solely through the deductive processes of the mind, not the fruits of manual labor. The inductive process came into existence through the contributions of Catholics Robert Grosseteste (c. 1168–1253), a Franciscan bishop and first chancellor of Oxford University, his student Roger Bacon (1214–1294), philosopher William of Occam (1285–1347), and Francis Bacon (1561–1626), who made records of experimental results after careful observation.[12]

Still today, the patronage of sciences by the Catholic Church continues through institutions like the Pontifical Academy of Sciences and the Vatican Observatory, with the continuation of their long-running contribution to science in astronomy and beyond by the Jesuits, who, with the document *Ratio Studiorum* (1599), sought to standardize the study of the sciences, along with Latin, Greek, classical literature, poetry, and philosophy, as well as non-European languages and arts. The Jesuits have been called "the single most important contributor to experimental physics in the seventeenth century."[13]

Even a cursory review of the history of science might serve as a quick reminder that the Catholic Church has led scientific discovery in many fields, and the Scientific Revolution was itself undertaken by people of faith, such as Kepler, Galileo, Pascal, and Newton. Groundbreaking ideas were developed by Catholics, like those of Nicolaus Copernicus (1473–1543) with heliocentrism and Jean-Baptiste Lamarck (1744–1829), whose Lamarckism foreshadowed the theory of evolution. Whole branches of science were founded or advanced dramatically by those who professed the Catholic faith, including Antoine Lavoisier (chemistry), Fr. Nicolas Steno (geology), Fr. Angelo Secchi (astrophysics), Gregor Mendel (genetics), and Fr. Georges Lemaître (cosmology).

Jonathan I. Lunine, PhD, the David C. Duncan Professor in the Physical Sciences of Cornell University and Director of the Cornell Center for Astrophysics and Planetary Science, finds that the rigorous pursuit of scientific truth paired with fidelity to revealed truth found in Catholic men and women throughout the ages is the best answer to the question of whether or not there is an inherent conflict between faith and science: "The lives of recent outstanding scientists who were also people of faith provide some of the most powerful arguments of all [that there is no conflict between science and faith]."[14]

Contributors of the Church to Scientific Advancement

Throughout history, Catholics have made many contributions to scientific inquiry. Here is a brief list of some of those contributions:

BLESSED HERMANN OF REICHENAU (1013–1054)
Astronomer

Reichenau's most important scientific contributions were in astronomy, but he also wrote on geometry, arithmetic, history, theology, and music theory.

SAINT HILDEGARD VON BINGEN (1098–1179)
Medicine and Natural History

Bingen wrote treatises on medicine and natural history and was a pharmacist, poet, composer, artist, hagiographer, and playwright. The theological writings of this mystic, visionary, and abbess made her a Doctor of the Church.

SAINT ALBERT THE GREAT (C. 1200–1280)
Philosopher and Natural Scientist

Albert was a bishop who wrote on philosophy, theology, botany, geography, astronomy, zoology, music, and physiology.

ROGER BACON (1219–1294)
The "Grandfather" of the Scientific Method

An English Franciscan and highly regarded academic, Roger Bacon, in concert with theology, studied mathematics, natural history, and light and optics. He was a forerunner of the scientific method, employing hypothesis, prediction, testing, and analysis, and he provided recommendations to Pope Clement IV for improving ecclesiastical studies (resulting in Bacon's *Opus Maius*, *Opus Minus*, and *Opus Tertiae*).

BISHOP ALBERT OF SAXONY (c. 1320–1390)
Logic and Natural Philosophy

Founder of the University of Vienna, and later serving as the bishop of Halberstadt, Albert is known for his contributions to the study of physics and, with Buridan (c. 1300–after 1358), developed the theory that was a precursor to the study of inertia.

NICOLAUS COPERNICUS (1473–1543)
Father of the Heliocentric Model of the Solar System

Challenging the traditional geocentric model of the solar system, Copernicus proposed a heliocentric model and remained a faithful Catholic. Beyond his interest in astronomy, he earned doctorates in both medicine and law and worked in finance.

FATHER CHRISTOPHER CLAVIUS (1538–1612)
Mathematician

This Catholic priest made contributions to algebra, geometry, astronomy, and cartography, and he worked on the reform of the Gregorian Calendar. As a longtime teacher at Collegio Roman, he influenced decades of students to spread scientific knowledge within the Jesuit Order and beyond through their missionary work.

FATHER BENEDETTO CASTELLI (1578–1643)
Fluid Mechanics

A Benedictine mathematician and longtime friend, supporter, and student of Galileo Galilei, Castelli wrote important works on fluids in motion.

FATHER BONAVENTURA CAVALIERI (1598–1647)
Optics and Motion

Cavalieri worked on the problems of optics and motion. His principle in geometry was a precursor of elements of integral calculus.

FATHER MARIN MERSENNE (1588–1648)
Father of Acoustics

This French priest and mathematician is known for Mersenne prime numbers and Mersenne's laws, which describe the harmonics of a vibrating string. His seminal work on music theory, *Harmonie universelle*, earned him the title of "father of acoustics."

BLESSED NICOLAS STENO (1638–1686)
Father of Modern Geology

This Danish bishop and father of geology wrote works that led to the fields of crystallography and paleontology, with his basic laws of stratigraphy helping to determine which dinosaurs came from which era, as well as calculating the approximate age of the earth. He also contributed significantly to the study of anatomy with discoveries of how the circulatory system works, where saliva comes from, and how muscles contract (including establishing that the heart is a muscle).

GIOVANNI (1700–1755) AND ANNA MORANDI MANZOLINI (1714–1774)
Anatomy

These Bolognese artists were well-known expert makers of wax anatomical models. Giovanni became a professor of anatomy at the University of Bologna, and their models were acquired by kings and popes.

ANTOINE LAVOISIER (1743–1794)
Father of Modern Chemistry

Antoine was a French nobleman and chemist whose significant influence on the field of chemistry was his changing of the science from a qualitative to a quantitative endeavor. Lavoisier is most noted for his discovery of the role oxygen plays in combustion.

FATHER ROGER BOSCOVICH (1711–1787)
Astronomy

A priest of the Society of Jesus who studied atomic theory, optics, math, physics, architecture, and astronomy, Father Boscovich used geometry to calculate planetary orbits. His book *A Theory of Natural Philosophy* was a landmark work in his day.

Father Angelo Secchi (1818–1878)
Pioneer of Astrophysics

Father Secchi was an Italian priest and astronomer who directed the observatory at the Pontifical Gregorian University for twenty-eight years. He was a pioneer in astronomical spectroscopy and was one of the first scientists to push the idea that the sun is a star.

Louis Pasteur (1822–1895)
Founder of Microbiology

This French chemist and microbiologist is best known for his discoveries of the principles of vaccination, microbial fermentation, and pasteurization. His work led to the understanding of the causes and preventions of diseases, setting the stage for standards of hygiene and public health.

Abbot Gregor Mendel (1822–1884)
Father of Genetics

Mendel was a meteorologist, mathematician, biologist, Augustinian friar, and abbot from the Austrian Empire (modern-day Czech Republic). Mendel's pea plant experiments conducted between 1856 and 1863 established many of the rules of heredity and resulted in Mendel coining the terms *recessive* and *dominant* in reference to certain traits and demonstrating the actions of invisible "factors" (now called genes).

FATHER GIUSEPPE MERCALLI (1850–1914)
Vulcanology

This Italian priest and seminary professor who studied volcanoes spent much of his life observing Vesuvius near Naples, where he taught at the University of Naples. He is the inventor of an alternative to the Richter scale for measuring the intensity of earthquakes.

FATHER HENRI BREUIL (1877–1961)
Archaeologist and Natural Scientist

Breuil was a French Jesuit priest and archaeologist, anthropologist, ethnologist, and geologist. He is renowned for his studies of cave art in the Somme and Dordogne valleys, as well as in Spain, Portugal, Italy, Ireland, and China.

FATHER GEORGES LEMAÎTRE (1894–1966)
Astronomer and Father of the Big Bang Theory

This Belgian Jesuit developed the groundbreaking proposition for the origins of the universe with his big bang theory, which states that the universe expanded from an initial point, which he called the primeval atom, running contrary to the prevailing theory that the universe was in a steady state. Father Lemaitre was a contemporary of Albert Einstein and collaborated with him often.

SISTER MIRIAM MICHAEL STIMSON (1913–2002)
Chemist

Sister Stimson was a member of the Adrian Dominican Sisters and a chemist. She is noted for her work on spectroscopy, and she played a role in the history of understanding DNA.

SISTER MARY KENNETH KELLER (1913–1985)
Pioneer in Computer Science

Sister Keller was an American member of the Sisters of Charity of the Blessed Virgin Mary. She was an educator and pioneer in computer science. She and Irving C. Tang were the first two people to earn a doctorate in computer science in the United States.

BLESSED JOSE GREGORIO HERNANDEZ (1864–1919)
Medical Doctor and Bacteriologist

This Venezuelan doctor on the path to sainthood treated the poor for free and was a respected scientist. He earned his medical degree in Venezuela before going on for further training and study in Paris. His writing and research on bacteriology, physiology, and philosophy has been published all over the world.

SAINT GIUSEPPE MOSCATI (1880–1927)
Medical Doctor and Chemist

Saint Giuseppe was a doctor who served the poor for free and one time risked his life during a volcanic eruption to rescue elderly patients. He was a pioneer in biochemistry and published research about diabetes treatments, leading to the use of insulin. He was among the early adopters of CPR, and his development of a more holistic approach and patient-centered methods influenced the field as a whole.

Blessed Guadalupe Ortiz (1916–1975)
Chemist and Research Scientist

As a chemistry PhD and professor, Blessed Guadalupe was one of the first female members of the Catholic lay organization Opus Dei. She established a mobile medical clinic for the poor and was an award-winning research scientist who died at the age of fifty-eight.

Venerable Jérôme Lejeune (1926–1994)
Pediatrician and Geneticist

Lejeune was a French pediatrician and geneticist who famously discovered that Down syndrome was caused by a duplicate chromosome 21. He identified several other chromosomal abnormality diseases, which lead to him receiving the world's highest genetics honor, the William Allen Award.

Faith in Science in a Secularized World

These members of the Catholic Church, and more, continue to impact the world of scientific thought and research through their legacies. The prevailing attitude of Catholic scientists for centuries is perhaps best represented by the prayer of astronomer Johann Kepler (1571–1630): "I thank you, Lord God our Creator, that you have allowed me to see the beauty in your work of creation."[15]

The Catholic Church continues to be an authority in matters of philosophy and theology and, through its well-established contributions over the centuries, has been a voice of significance in science in an earlier era as well. With the gradual secularization of the West, however, the influence of the Church over scientific research has gradually waned. Now, in this modern age, with its role and impact having been diminished, the Church has not abandoned science or attempted to distance itself from scientific thought. Instead, the Catholic Church turns to science in a way that continues to far supersede any other faith-based institution. In addition to continuing the work of the Vatican Observatory and sponsoring various projects of the Pontifical Academy of Sciences, which gathers both Catholic and secular experts in their fields, the Catholic Church uses the tools and technologies of science in an effort to examine and exclude claims of the miraculous—whether it be the investigation into medical cures seemingly without natural explanation or claims of supernatural phenomena like weeping statues and Eucharistic miracles. The relationship between the Catholic Church and science has evolved but forges ahead.

With this foundation laid, let us turn now to some of these miraculous events.

2

A Church of Miracles

What Exactly Is a Miracle?

This seems like a fair question to ask before we discuss various types of miracles and how the Church goes about examining and considering them. Deriving from the Latin word *mirari*—"to be amazed"— *miracle* is a term given to occurrences that are without natural explanation and go beyond normal human experience and power, thus implying divine intervention. Miracles are seen as blessings rendering beneficial results. This is a key element of a miracle, since something that is supernatural that is *not* good cannot be of God, and something that is merely inexplicable (but is not seen as a blessing) is considered a mystery, or a marvel. These special moments go beyond our expectations and leave us, indeed, amazed.

Arguably the greatest theologian in Church history, Saint Thomas Aquinas, in his *Summa Contra Gentiles*, defines a miracle as something inexplicable with an unknowable cause attributable only to God. According to Thomas's organizational system, first degree miracles are divine acts beyond the capability of nature, such as Jesus turning water into wine. In the second degree are those things done by God within the realm of nature but accomplished in an unnatural way. When a person walks, it is natural but not when they have been permanently paralyzed. Finally, third degree miracles are also done by God but beyond what nature can do running its normal course. Some illnesses are liable to go away on their own, but an instantaneous cure may rightly be considered miraculous. All these sorts of miracles will be discussed in due time.

Of course, the world owns its fair share of doubters. Famed atheist David Hume argued that "miracles are impossible because miracles can't happen," while Richard Dawkins, in his popular book *The God Delusion*, suggested that "miracles, by definition, violate the principles of science."

Skeptics like them and their disciples may dismiss miracles as fanciful notions of the uneducated and superstitious, but they still must provide an explanation for the inexplicable. More often than not, they can provide no such explanation.

A Faith Founded Upon Miracles

We learn of miracles in the Bible, both in the Old Testament, where God uses them to make his divine will manifest, and in the New Testament, where Jesus uses them to establish his divinity in an incontrovertible way. With his miracles, Jesus healed the sick, raised the dead, cast out demons, and demonstrated his power over nature, each miracle along the way foreshadowing what would be his ultimate miracle, proving him to be divine: his victory over death. Our belief in the story of Christianity rests on the two great supernatural events of the Incarnation and the Resurrection, but every hour of every day, all around the world, the faithful put their belief in Catholicism's greatest miracle: the transformation of bread and wine into the body and blood of Jesus Christ, which takes place at the Sacred Mass.

Miracles have always bolstered and enlivened the faith of believers. Throughout the Old Testament, beginning with the Genesis account of creation, we see numerous signs and wonders demonstrating God's favor or punishment. In the time of Christ, miracles served as proofs of his divinity, such that without them, he is seen as just a great moral teacher. Jesus cast out demons, healed the sick from their infirmities, raised people from the dead, changed water into wine, multiplied loaves and fishes to feed the multitude, and walked on water. There are thirty-seven biblical miracles of Jesus that we know of, but as Saint John states, "There are also many other things that Jesus did, but if these were to be described individually, I do not think the whole world would contain the books that would be written" (Jn 21:25).

Miracles helped establish the young Church when the apostles were given the mandate by Christ to work wonders in his name. The apostles continued to see visions and perform miracles in his name after his death: curing illnesses, helping the lame to walk, and casting out demons. Saint Peter's shadow and Saint Paul's handkerchiefs were even said to be imbued with spiritual powers so great that they healed the sick (see Acts 5:15–16; 19:12).

The Roman emperor Constantine changed the course of history when he legalized Christianity in the year 312 after experiencing a vision in the sky of the IHS Christogram, telling him,

"In this sign, conquer." And throughout history, saints have wrought the power of God, demonstrating their connection with him, and received inspiration through divine messages.

Throughout Christian history, Servites, Mercedarians, and numerous other religious orders have been the result of the supernatural experiences of their founders, and some of the most beautiful churches in Christendom, including five of the largest twelve places of worship (by square footage), were inspired by a vision of the Virgin Mary. Huge numbers of the faithful, including twenty million a year at Guadalupe, five million at Fatima, and four million at Lourdes, go on pilgrimage to the sites of miracles all over the world. Millions of conversions are credited to the events on Tepeyac Hill in 1531 when Our Lady of Guadalupe appeared to Saint Juan Diego. Conversions are also credited to the Miraculous Medal and other devotions that have resulted from miraculous beginnings. Even the most famous of all sacramentals—the rosary—comes from the pious tradition that Saint Dominic received a thirteenth-century vision of the Virgin Mary, imploring him to preach about her Rosary to defeat the Albigensian heresy.

Indeed, this brief (and incomplete) review of the Church's promotion of and reliance on miracles shows how we live amidst a faith founded on miracles.

Public Revelation vs. Private Revelation

And yet, for all the emphasis that the Catholic Church seems to place on miracles, belief even in approved miracles is not required as a matter of faith. For example, if someone were to believe that Saint Juan Diego's tilma, with the image of Our Lady of Guadalupe on it, was merely a human creation, he could hold to that opinion and still be a good Catholic. Likewise, if another were to say the healing miracles that occur in the waters of Lourdes—as many as seven thousand considered remarkable cures and seventy considered to be without natural explanation—were not true miracles because science doesn't yet know what it doesn't know, he could still be a Catholic in good standing. Similarly, if someone were to believe that the visionaries of Fatima were just children with active imaginations, he could in clear conscience still call himself a faithful Catholic.

There are plenty of facts available to counter each of those naturalistic arguments, but nonetheless, these occurrences belong to the realm of private revelation. Such things revealed to saintly individuals after the death of Saint John the Evangelist and outside of the Gospels do not complete the public revelation given to us in Scripture and Tradition. Miracles are not a substitute for absolute faith in God. The centrality of the Catholic faith can be found in the final revelation given to the world in the person, acts, and words of Jesus Christ. The working of miracles is not intended to satisfy people's curiosity or desire for magic.[16] Pope Francis has emphasized this, saying that God is not "a magician with a magic wand."

Miracles often inspire the faithful to move toward a deeper relationship with Christ, but the Church protects its members from dubious and even dangerous alleged supernatural events by carrying out serious scientific investigations into credible miraculous claims and, from this, recommending how specific cases should be dealt with.

It has always been important for the faithful to know if miracles in question are in fact authentic. But the process of validation has changed over the years. In an earlier age, when scientific examination had not been developed and a thorough investigation by expert authorities was not deemed necessary, prayerful discernment by a bishop or priest, in concert with a local community, constituted the entirety of the effort to ascertain whether a miracle had indeed occurred. Today, as we will soon see, that process has become more scientific and formulized.

Examining the Message

It is important to distinguish between miracles that do not involve explicit divine messages, like healings, weeping statues, and Eucharistic phenomena, and those that are accompanied by visions or messages. While the former can carry great meaning for those who experience them and are undoubtedly signs with great *unspoken* meaning, they do not come with direct messages from heaven that the Church must interpret.

When such messages *are* present through private revelation, there is the added complication of the messages potentially contradicting, or at least challenging, what we read in public revelation or are taught through the teaching of the Magisterium. Special attention must be given, and at times quick action taken, by Church authorities in order that people are not deceived by these events, which can be accompanied by false theology and financial impropriety.

Perhaps the first significant instance of divine locutions that Rome chose to investigate was those of Saint Bridget of Sweden, one of history's greatest mystics and patron saints of Europe. Her revelations were reportedly infused instantaneously to her, before being dictated to priests, who transcribed her words and translated them into Latin. These messages covered a wide range of topics: from doing laundry well to the next strategic move the pope should take during the Crusades! With some of her visions touching on matters that impacted the Catholic Church as a whole, the Vatican began to investigate the content of her messages at the Council of Constance (1414–1418) and the Council of Basle (1431–1449). This helped to create the precedence for how divine messages should be considered and studied.

At the Fifth Lateran Council (1512–1517), called by Pope Julius II, with the proliferation of similar claims of private revelation being made throughout the world, it was determined that the Vatican would handle all such claims of the supernatural, reserving approval of new prophecies and revelations to Rome and Rome alone. However, the Council of Trent (1545–1563) returned investigations to the local level. This was due either to the sheer volume of reported miracles being proposed to Rome or to the concept of subsidiarity, an element of Catholic social teaching which states that matters should be handled by the smallest, lowest, or least centralized authority. (In other words, political decisions should be made by local authorities, then state, then federal, only rising to the next level if it is absolutely necessary.)

Under this new structure, authorized bishops render judgments after rigorously investigating the claim, using science (including in modern times potentially evaluating brain scans and other cognitive testing in the hopes of revealing and understanding the brain activity of the alleged visionary) and conducting interviews, along with prayerful discernment. Throughout the entire process, the seer's credibility is put on trial and the content of the messages are examined to determine whether or not they are in harmony with Church teaching.

The current guidelines for the judgment of apparition claims were laid out in a recent Congregation for the Doctrine of the Faith (CDF) document called the *Normae Congregationis de Modo Procedendi in Diudicandis Praesumptis Apparitionibus ac Revelationibus* ("Norms of the Congregation for Proceeding in Judging Alleged Apparitions and Revelations") and approved by Pope Paul VI on February 27, 1978. It was written *sub secreto*, for the eyes of bishops alone, but was made public in 2012.

According to this document and canon law, the competent authority is the local bishop, who may make a public judgment on the authenticity of a miracle claim with no requirement to secure Vatican commentary. Although the diocesan bishop possesses the right to initiate an investigation, that country's national conference of bishops can subsequently intervene at his request or at the request of a qualified group of faithful. If necessary, the Vatican can then also intervene if the situation involves the Church at large or if discernment requires it.

A classic example that shows this progression of intervening authorities is the controversial alleged apparitions of Medjugorje. This story involves the famed long-running phenomena of six children in Bosnia-Herzegovina being visited by the Virgin Mary. These visits, which began in 1981, were first investigated and discouraged by the local ordinary but were later examined by the 1991 Zadar Commission of the

Yugoslavian bishops and then reevaluated by a Vatican commission formed in 2010. While no formal ruling has yet been made by the Congregation for the Doctrine of the Faith or the pope, the commission report has been informally commented on by Pope Francis and leaked to the internet. The conclusion of the report seems to suggest that the first nine apparitions were authentic while the thousands occurring over the course of over forty years have mixed reviews and spark many questions. Our purposes here are not to comment one way or the other on Medjugorje but to simply show the process by which cases can rise up the Church ladder.

Typically, if the situation merits it, the bishop will seek a report from an assembled commission of experts, such as theologians, psychologists, psychiatrists, Mariologists, or anthropologists. They assess the phenomena and the people who report them, looking for evidence of authenticity. Next, they are to study any messages that are associated with the extraordinary reports to ascertain whether they conform to Church teaching. The third question raised by the document appraises the pastoral implications of the phenomena by studying the impact of the reported apparitions. Miraculous physical healings, conversions, vocations, and a return to the sacraments are considered good fruits.

There are three categories of apparition judgments that relate most importantly to the supernatural character of the event. These are:

1. *constat de non supernaturalitate*
2. *non constat de supernaturalitate*
3. *constat de supernaturalitate*

The first asserts that the event is *not* worthy of belief, demonstrated by the Latin formulation *constat de non supernaturalitate*; that is, "It is established as not supernatural." The negative criteria include errors in the facts of the case or in doctrinal attributions to Jesus or Mary, the pursuit of financial gain, and psychological disorders in the visionary. A disobedience to Church guidance and a lack of humility can be common red flags as well.

In a modern case easily ruled a hoax, Bishop Michael Olson of the Catholic diocese of Fort Worth released a statement in August 2019 declaring that the alleged apparitions, messages, and miracles under the name Mystical Rose–Our Lady of Argyle were "fabricated." The alleged visionary was caught on security camera leaving behind roses that were claimed to have miraculously appeared. Moreover, the Marian statue that was said to be bleeding was examined by a local artist who assessed it as being latex body paint with visible brush marks present.

A second category of judgment, *non constat*, states that an event is "not established as supernatural." Notice the subtle but important difference in meaning between "it is established as not supernatural" and "not established as supernatural." This stance is one of uncertainty, calling for a wait-and-see approach. The vast majority of investigated apparitions receive this assessment when the investigative committee cannot at that time make a definitive conclusion. An apparition with such a designation may or may not be of supernatural origin. While there is no proof of the phenomenon originating from anything but natural causes, none of the negative criteria are fulfilled and the supernatural cause is not ruled out.

Finally, in extremely rare cases, an event is established as supernatural, *constat de supernaturalitate.* There must be moral certainty or at least great probability of the miracle occurring, the visionary and the content of the revelations must be evaluated positively, and there must be healthy devotion with good spiritual fruits that flow from it. When an apparition is approved, the Virgin Mary can be venerated in a special way at the site, but it often takes decades or longer for a local bishop to issue a definitive statement.

In one extreme case, the 1664 visions reported by Benedicta Rencurel in Le Laus, France, were finally validated in 2008. In the only such example in the United States, Bishop David L. Ricken of Green Bay initiated an investigation where a team of three renowned Mariologists examined the merits of the 1859 claims of Adele Brise, a Belgian farm worker who reported that she saw the Blessed Virgin Mary on three occasions and began to spread her messages of conversion and catechesis. After the commission concluded, Ricken declared in 2010 that there was enough evidence to declare with confidence that these supernatural events were "worthy of belief" and contained nothing contrary to the teachings of the Church.

While not required for an apparition or other miracle to be considered approved, occasionally the Vatican will provide another layer of recognition by releasing an official document, constructing or elevating a basilica, canonizing a visionary, establishing a feast day, or simply having the pope visit that location with a special Marian prayer or with a symbolic golden rose. Only twenty-eight times since the Council of Trent has a local bishop declared an apparition to be worthy of belief, and of those, only sixteen have received additional recognition from the Vatican. This shows us that the Church approaches miraculous claims of divine revelations with skepticism since there have been over 2,500 claims of Marian apparitions.

Miracles Without Explicit Messages

Returning to those miracles void of messages, the Church also has guidelines in place to determine credibility. Some of these rules were developed by the Italian cardinal Prospero Lambertini (1675–1758), the future Benedict XIV, who provided guidance for the evaluation of healing miracles needed with the canonization of saints in *De Servorum Dei Beatificatione et de Beatorum Canonizatione.* In this treatise, he insisted that reason must be used to determine whether the miracles being claimed are truly beyond ordinary human experience and without natural cause. The standards he established for the judgment of healing miracles became known as the Lambertini criteria and are still in use today by the International Lourdes Medical Committee and Medical Commission of the Congregation for the Causes of Saints.

While miracles of healing seem to generate interest amongst people of all faiths, the Catholic Church is the only religion that considers most other alleged miraculous phenomena in its examinations, partly because the Eucharist, relics, the Virgin Mary, and the rite of recognition (whereby a saint's tomb is opened) all belong almost exclusively to the Catholic belief system.

Different miracle types require different forms of attention in investigations by the Church. Perhaps the clearest cases are those where science carries the most weight in evaluating the authenticity of the event. In reports of Eucharistic miracles, where the host is said to have physically turned into bleeding flesh, the wafer is typically secured by authorities at the instruction of the local bishop in order to perform scientific tests that can ferret out a hoax from an authentic miracle. In some extremely rare cases, actual human blood or heart muscle has been found within the host, including a 1996 example in Argentina positively verified by then archbishop Jorge Mario Bergoglio, the future Pope Francis.

Investigations of weeping icons also employ science to uncover trickery or natural explanations, like leaky duct work in a church building. In one case from 1953 that was documented on film, Pope Pius XII declared on Vatican Radio the statue of the Weeping Madonna of Syracuse, Italy, to be an authentic miracle of lachrymation. The statue, given to a young couple as a wedding gift, passed scientific scrutiny and wrought hundreds of verified miracles, including the restoration of sight to the woman who owned the statue. Other statues, like the one of Our Lady of Akita in 1973 (Japan), have been verified by scientists to produce human blood. (We will come to that topic shortly.)

Alleged cases of the stigmata—that is, those people mystically exhibiting the wounds of Christ in their hands, feet, and forehead—rely heavily on thorough medical examinations to rule out fraud. The most famous modern stigmatic, Saint Pio, a Capuchin monk from Pietrelcina, Italy, with many purported mystical gifts, underwent medical tests and scrutiny in silence while the Church verified these extraordinary events. The number, location, and size of the wounds of stigmatics varies widely, suggesting that a person with stigmata at least in part experiences the passion of Christ according to his personal understanding of it.

In all such claims of miraculous phenomena like these, modern technology presents a double-edged sword in the debate over credibility. Scientific developments have expanded our knowledge of the human body and all its functions, helping us discern natural explanations when they are present and, in other cases, helping us expose a fraud. But other advances make it easier than ever to fake video and audio evidence, casting suspicion on any supposed evidence of the supernatural and calling into question what is true and what is not.

Nonetheless, contrary to the opinion of Cessationists, who would argue that all miracles ceased after the Bible had been written, supernatural events still abound in today's world. Cases of Marian apparitions, Eucharistic miracles, weeping statues, and inexplicable healings continue to be reported with regularity. And the Church, after rigorously examining and rendering judgment on these major supernatural occurrences, embraces those that bear the authentic mark of God working in our world. These miracles and others have played a major role in the growth of the Catholic Church.

That being said, not every blessing warrants a full investigation by a Vatican commission. It is to this topic that we will now turn to see what criteria is used in determining what to investigate and what to leave alone.

3

When the Church
Does Not Investigate

The Phenomenon of Pareidolia

As we demonstrated in the last chapter, the Catholic Church turns to science to investigate several different kinds of miracles. But to keep from giving the impression that the Church leaps at every mystical phenomenon reported somewhere and anywhere in the world, a few instances should be highlighted of the many (many, many) reports of miraculous occurrences in which the Church does *not* conduct an investigation.

Take, for example, "Our Lady of the Underpass," a stain vaguely resembling an artistic depiction of the Blessed Mother found beneath the Kennedy Expressway along Fullerton Avenue in Chicago in 2005. The only investigation that was conducted here was that done by curious citizens rather than Church authorities. The Illinois Department of Transportation deemed it to be a stain caused by salt runoff.[17]

The "Clearwater Virgin" was another case of a Guadalupe-colored image of the Virgin Mary manifesting itself in the glass façade of a finance building in Clearwater, Florida. This attracted an estimated one million visitors over the next several years. A local chemist examined the windows and suggested the stain was produced by water deposits, perhaps from a nearby water sprinkler, which combined with weathering to yield a chemical reaction like that often seen on old bottles.[18]

There have been numerous instances of images like this inviting the phenomenon of pareidolia—the brain's false perception of imagery based on familiar patterns. Many have been looked at scientifically but not with Church-sanctioned efforts. The Church simply cannot get involved every time someone thinks they see angels in the clouds. Too often it may be a coincidence, or a fraud, or perhaps it just doesn't actually look like much at all.

Unverifiable Miracles and Other Occurrences

In addition to these cases of pareidolia, there are claims all around the world of miracles and unexplained events that cannot be investigated by science because a direct cause-and-effect relationship cannot be established.

One such case comes three hours northeast of Clearwater, in St. Augustine, where the popular pilgrimage site of the National Shrine of Our Lady of La Leche at Nombre de Dios, founded in 1587, is located. This is perhaps the first Marian shrine in the continental United States. It is frequented by Catholic faithful who wish to honor alleged miracles that have not been formally investigated by Church authorities. The focal point of the shrine is a statue of the Virgin Mary nursing the child Jesus. Part of the reason for the popularity of the pilgrimage site is the history of beautiful stories of visitors seeking her intercession for successful pregnancy and delivery. The shrine keeps on file the testimonies and medical reports related to these blessings, but none thus far have warranted the Church's involvement.

Traveling west, many miracles in New Orleans have been recorded and attributed to the intercession of the Virgin Mary under the title of Our Lady of Prompt Succor, a name that refers to a wonder-working statue of the Madonna and Child that received a canonical coronation from Pope Leo XIII in 1895. The feast day is celebrated locally on January 8, the date of one of the two major miraculous stories retold there.

In 1812, Our Lady of Prompt Succor was invoked by the Ursuline Sisters while a devastating fire in New Orleans advanced on the convent. A miracle indeed, the convent was one of the few buildings spared from destruction. Three years later in 1815, New Orleans residents joined the Ursuline sisters at their convent to pray throughout the night for the help of Our Lady of Prompt Succor. General Andrew Jackson's six thousand American troops went on to defeat fifteen thousand British soldiers on the plains of Chalmette in the Battle of New Orleans. An annual Mass of Thanksgiving has been held on January 8 ever since.

Moving even farther west, we will find a famed New Mexico curiosity, considered by some to be a miracle. The Loretto Chapel is best known for its "miraculous" spiral staircase—popularly called the St. Joseph Staircase—that has been lauded for its design and master craftsmanship, which rises twenty feet to the choir loft while making two full turns, all without the support of a central pole, and held together with wooden pegs and glue rather than metal hardware. According to local legend, when the nuns there realized they needed a new staircase to reach the choir loft of their newly remodeled chapel, they welcomed the services of a mysterious carpenter, who arrived uninvited and left in silence, without pay, after creating the aforementioned remarkable staircase that continues to baffle and impresses modern engineers. Some testing by dendrologists has been done to determine the exact wood used to construct the staircase, but it remains unknown, other than being confirmed as type of spruce, probably non-native to New Mexico.[19]

Stories like these, though no doubt true in many ways, bleed into the category of pious legend, stories from another era that are too far gone to be documented or investigated. And even if they occurred more recently, there is no way to scientifically prove that Mary's intercession aided Jackson's troops, or diverted the flames of a fire, or that Saint Joseph himself built that remarkable staircase, or that a statue in St. Augustine was the cause of an unexpected and joyous pregnancy. Those who believe these things believe them through faith.

While the Church does not rule on the authenticity of such claims, they do encourage devotions like Our Lady of La Leche and Our Lady of Prompt Succor (and many similar devotions to Saint Joseph) as an aide to our faith. The faithful do not so much place their trust in the event that supposedly took place as they do in the Lady (or the saint) who is said to have brought these miraculous events about through the power of God. It is the same way with the relic of a saint; devotees are not venerating the relic itself but the person to whom the relic is attached. Here, the story itself is not held up but rather the one who inspired belief through these stories. In a sense, the authenticity of such stories is almost irrelevant in seeking holiness. The Catholic Church encourages faith in God, his Church, and the saints and angels as being what truly matters. If these stories strengthen one's faith, then they are to be appreciated, but they should not be required for belief. This is a theme we will return to again and again because it is so important to understand.

Recurring Miracles with Fragile Artifacts

Another kind of legend that cannot be verified is when a relic or sacred object claims to be tied to something pertaining to the life of Jesus or Mary or a certain saint. Claims abound of pieces of the true cross, or Mary's veil, or in one case, the *Sacra Spina*, the "Holy Thorn," of Andria, Italy, which is said to be from the true crown of thorns of Jesus Christ. This single thorn is kept safe as part of a reliquary, protruding three inches from the top of a silver encasement adorned with two golden angels.

Each of these sacred objects come with elaborate and often credible backstories for how we come to believe in the truth of their origin. But only on seldom occasions can such a story be authenticated with any assurance. The Church cannot untangle history that is lost to humanity or uncover proof that is not there.

However, some of these sacred objects do offer what seems to be their own proof of their miraculous origins. According to tradition, the *Sacra Spina* will "bleed" or sweat when the feasts of Good Friday and the Annunciation fall on the same day (meaning, when Good Friday falls on March 25, the feast of the Annunciation). The last such occurrence like this took place on March 25, 2016 with Bishop Raffaele Calabro, bishop emeritus of Andria, confirming that the thorn began to bleed. A commission that observes the phenomena confirmed the formation of three spherical formations, or small whitish "gems," on the thorn at 4:50 p.m., close to the time of our Lord's passion and crucifixion, and noted "on the base of the thorn is the residue of the preceding miracle of 2005." The first recorded occurrence of this took place in 1633, and the next coincidence of dates will be in 2157.[20]

A similar phenomenon is the centuries-old repeating liquefaction of the blood of Saint Januarius (San Gennaro) in Naples, Italy. Every September 19, the feast day of this third-century bishop-martyr and patron saint of Naples, the faithful of the city gather in the Naples cathedral with hopes of seeing a miracle happen. (The blood is also said to liquefy two other times each year: December 16, for the anniversary of Naples's preservation from the 1631 eruption of Mount Vesuvius, and in the afternoon of the first Saturday in May, in remembrance of the unification of Saint Januarius's relics.) The archbishop of Naples will stand before the congregation and pray over the saint's blood, which is held in an ampoule, a hermetically sealed almond-shaped glass reliquary. He will first demonstrate that it is solid (having hardened with time), but after some variable amount of time, he will hold it up horizontally to display for all to see the blood having changed states from solid to liquid. Thousands of attendees of the Mass celebrate the liquefaction with raucous cheers. This event is met with jubilation because, on the very rare occasion when it does not liquefy, they see it as a harbinger of problems for their city: the eruption of Mount Vesuvius, disease outbreaks, and financial collapse have been just some of the events marked by years without the sacred sign. For the first time in the presence of a pope in 150 years—the blood last liquefied in 1848 for Pius IX—the phenomena occurred with Pope Francis at the cathedral on March 21, 2015.

Some speculative studies have been carried out through the years, including the 1902 spectroscopic analysis (the use of light to investigate the composition and physical structure of matter) of Italian scientist Gennaro Sperindeo, which reported the spectrum being consistent with hemoglobin.[21] Some scientists, like Luigi Garlaschelli, have proposed that the substance may not in fact be blood but instead a photosensitive, hygroscopic, or low-melting point thixotropic gel[22] exhibiting changes in viscosity corresponding to variation in movement, like hydrated iron oxide, $FeO\,(OH)$, easily available in ancient times.[23]

In 2010, a molecular biologist named Giuseppe Geraci from Frederick II University in Naples, while claiming some success in reproducing the phenomena with other blood samples, still admitted, "There is no univocal scientific fact that explains why these changes take place. It is not enough to attribute to the movement the ability to dissolve the blood, the liquid contained in the Treasure case changes state for reasons still to be identified."[24]

The Church has not commented on any of these studies, nor the ones who support the authenticity of the miracle, nor the ones who seek to disprove it. It is not the Church's place to evaluate the claims of anyone who performs a study or gives an opinion about such a matter (there are many such opinions), and little would be accomplished if she did. Nor has the Church sponsored any scientific investigations on the actual substance inside the reliquary for fear of causing irreparable damage. This is an important factor that must be considered when proposing to study an ancient artifact: is it worth the risk of destroying it? Will a study reveal enough beneficial information to outweigh that risk? More often than not, the Church says not.

Rome has always been supportive of the local Neapolitan celebrations, as well as other similar events tied to sacred objects. But the support the Church gives to these events is more tied to the strengthening of a congregation or community's faith, drawing them into churches where they hear the Word of God and receive the Eucharist and where they can ask for the intercession of the saints and for miracles to be worked in their own lives. The miraculous event is, ironically, somewhat secondary. That being said, for all the skeptics who think these sorts of recurring miracles are a hoax, one might ask how they seem to occur only on certain days tied to important feasts on the liturgical calendar. If the phenomenon were the result of random scientific influences, that would not explain the timing. Furthermore, hundreds, if not thousands, of witnesses are there to watch. Such a hoax would be difficult to carry out with that many witnesses present.

Miracles Outside the Church's "Jurisdiction"

There are other seemingly miraculous events that the Roman Catholic Church has not investigated because they fall within the purview of Eastern Christian Churches.

For example, beginning on April 2, 1968, the Virgin Mary reportedly appeared, without words, hovering above St. Mark's Coptic Church and visible to large crowds sporadically for a span of three years. The appearances were reported on many occasions, especially at night, and sometimes they were accompanied by glowing white doves that would fly around her. These occurrences took place two or three times a week until 1971 and attracted sometimes up to 250,000 people, with an estimated 40 million people in total witnessing these events. Christians, Jews, Muslims, and unbelievers gathered to view the sight. The apparitions were photographed, filmed, and broadcast on Egyptian TV. The Coptic Church—after much prayerful discernment, but no scientific testing—approved the apparitions, but the Catholic Church has never commented on it officially.

A similar situation concerns "the Holy Fire," an annual event attended by thousands of pilgrims and local Christians of all denominations who gather in Jerusalem to witness something that Orthodox Christians view as miraculous. This event takes place at the Church of the Holy Sepulcher on the day before the Orthodox Easter, known as Great Saturday (Holy Saturday). Orthodox tradition holds that the "Holy Fire" can be seen as a blue light that emanates from the tomb of Jesus Christ, rising from the marble slab covering the stone bed where our Lord's body was laid to rest. The light is said to resemble a column of fire. Surrounded by an approving and jubilant crowd, the patriarch comes out with the two candles lit, which are then used to light candles held by the other clergy and pilgrims in attendance. The fire supposedly also spontaneously lights other lamps and candles around the church.

The Holy Fire is then taken to Greece by special flight and similarly to other countries with major Orthodox populations and received by church and state leaders.

There have been no scientific tests that verify this claim, and many have disputed the alleged miraculous descent of the fire as a financially motivated hoax. Some skeptics have sought to debunk the phenomenon by demonstrating in a televised test that candles could be spontaneously ignited after approximately twenty minutes due to the self-ignition properties of white phosphorus when in contact with air. Whatever the case, the Catholic Church has not speculated about the authenticity of such a claim since they did not take place in the Church's "jurisdiction." It is not the Church's place to investigate and comment on miracles occurring within other faiths, even ones in close communion with Rome.

These are but some of the many purportedly miraculous phenomena for which the Catholic Church does not initiate any scientific investigation for various reasons that hopefully are now clear. This was an important step in our investigation because in understanding the phenomena that the Church does not investigate or comment on, we can better understand those things she does make determinations on and then show the process of how such investigations are carried out. Let us turn now to some of those miracles. First, let us examine miraculous healings.

4

Healing Miracles

Does Prayer Help?

When an inexplicable miracle of healing takes place, some people speculate that the mind has the ability to heal the body through psychosomatic effects and auto-suggestion rather than believe something miraculous took place. They do not question whether or not prayer can help, only the way in which it helps, seeing it not as a means to receive divine assistance but as a way to support and engage the mind, which in turn can assist the body.

According to the book *Nothing Short of a Miracle* by Patricia Treece, numerous studies have been run that consider and measure the effects one's faith can have on physical healings. Duke University, Fordham University, Agnes Scott College, the Institute for Psychobiological Research (London), and UCLA have all conducted studies that have shown that prayer can have positive effects on the human body, including on blood cell count, skin temperature, blood pressure, and brain waves.[25] Other clinical trials have demonstrated a correlation in elderly patients who pray during the first year after coronary artery bypass surgery and experience less depression and anxiety, factors that influence recovery time.[26] One 2002 study reported in the *Annals of Behavioral Medicine* linked the length of time AIDS patients survived to the amount they prayed.[27]

Again, some may see prayer simply as a way to give a little "pep talk" to the mind to keep it thinking positively so that it can find ways to help heal the body. That would not explain, though, how patients also seem to do better when *others* pray for them. Miraculous cures of infants would be one example, such as the Vatican-validated case of the return to life of a stillborn child, who went without breathing for sixty-one minutes in September 2010, through the intercession of Venerable Fulton Sheen. Clearly, this young child was not aided by his own prayers. Furthermore, researchers at Saint Luke's Hospital in Kansas City released a study that found that coronary care unit patients who received intercessory prayer, even without their knowledge, suffered fewer complications than those patients who were not prayed for.[28]

How would the skeptic explain these?

It seems that heavenly intervention can have an effect on the healing of the body both in ordinary and extraordinary ways. It is to the latter that we will turn next.

The Congregation for the Causes of Saints

It may surprise some to know that the Vatican does not deploy a team of miracle investigators when credible reports of medical miracles occur. The spontaneous healing of a stage-4 cancer victim or the recovery of eyesight for a blind person will not result in a team of cassock-wearing gentleman knocking on your door. The Church encourages a spirit of gratitude to God for such miracles, but there would be no resulting activity on their part. At least most of the time. There are, of course, exceptions. Most Catholics have heard of the Congregation for the Causes of Saints. This council examines medical miracles proposed by the postulators of canonization causes. (Postulators are those who head up the cause for someone's sainthood.) Their methods involve a multi-stage, centuries-old process of investigation, with years of meticulous research and dozens, if not hundreds, of interviews. The eighteenth-century criteria used by the medical commission of the congregation employs the same Lambertini criteria discussed in a previous chapter.

According to these rules, the healing must be *spontaneous*, *complete*, and *permanent*, and cannot be produced by another crisis (or disease) that would make it possible that the cure was wholly or partially natural. No medical treatment must have been given, or it must be certain that the treatment given had no connection to the cure. Cases where a medical intervention has unsuccessfully been attempted already or prior to a surgery, for example, are the likeliest cases to be considered by Rome. When the healing is deemed miraculous, it advances the cause for canonization for the holy man or woman in question.

In the sainthood process, there are four stages in a non-martyrdom case. First, a worthy candidate for consideration is named a servant of God. After years of scrutiny, fact-finding, and gathering testimonies of witnesses and experts, a *positio* (an academic position paper oftentimes several hundred pages in length) is written by the cause for canonization and submitted to the Congregation for the Causes of Saints at the Vatican. The long process of evaluation, now usually a decade or two in typical cases, in an earlier era might have taken a century or more. After a positive vote by the congregation, the pope will then decide to promulgate a decree stating the person in question lived a life of heroic virtue, thus declaring the candidate to be venerable.

The faithful may then seek the intercession of the potential saint in the hopes of a miracle. This is one factor in the process that is often overlooked. Only once the designation of venerable has been declared may any miracles be submitted to Rome for consideration. If they are submitted, they are seen as an important indicator of sainthood, a divine confirmation of a candidate's worthiness for the next two stages: beatification and canonization. When the Vatican investigates a miracle allegedly worked through the intercession of a would-be saint to validate that they are in heaven with God interceding for the faithful, the same Lambertini criteria is applied.

Almost all of the miracles considered for sainthood causes—99 percent—are medical healings. This is mostly because official documentation exists both before and after the event in question. Initially, medical experts on the diocesan level assess a case and sift through all the clinical evidence before and after the cure. On the local level, the investigation is spearheaded by an uninvolved (unbiased) doctor appointed by the bishop. The doctors who treated the patient do not need to believe in Christianity or even in the reality of miracles, but they must have established both that the condition was without hope for recovery, with all appropriate treatments and up-to-date medical care having failed, and also that the subsequent faith-based recovery from certain death or permanent disability had nothing to do with them. When these criteria are met (which is rare), a *Positio Super Miraculo* is written, meticulously documenting the miracle. It is then sent via the postulator to the Vatican's Congregation for the Causes of Saints.

The medical commission—or *Consulta Medica*—for the Congregation for the Causes of Saints features over sixty international doctors in various specialties and faith backgrounds. For those who are wondering, there is evidence of the Catholic Church relying on non-practicing Catholic and non-Catholic doctors since the Middle Ages.[29] These medical experts are not tasked with judging whether the cure is miraculous—only if there is a natural explanation—and don't need to answer the question if it is a case of causation or coincidence. Applying the Lambertini criteria, they must determine if the purported cure is an instance of misdiagnosis, is related to an applied treatment, or if the disease simply ran its course naturally.

Medical miracles by themselves are difficult to validate with so many strict guidelines, but in canonization causes, an additional difficulty lies in that the prayers to a potential saint must be directed *exclusively* to that singular person (not to other saints or potential saints in addition). This is another factor that often gets forgotten or overlooked, or misunderstood by the faithful as they push for canonizations.

Yet another aspect of the investigation that gets overlooked is the permanence of the cure. In the beatification miracle of Saint Katharine Drexel (1858–1955) of Philadelphia, Rome examined the cure of a boy named Robert Gutherman who had lost hearing in one ear due to a serious infection that ate away the bones in his ear. Despite his hearing having returned after the family's prayers to the saintly nun, and the bones in his ear having been miraculously restored, Gutherman's hearing was examined well into adulthood to establish the permanence of the cure. That Vatican-validated cure inspired the prayers in another case of hearing loss when two-year-old Amy Wall was miraculously healed in 1994 of nerve deafness through then-Blessed Katharine Drexel's intercession. The investigation resulted in a seven-hundred-page *positio* covering the lifetime medical history of the girl, interviews with doctors, testimonies from friends and relatives about the details of her condition and the speed of her recovery, and the specifics of how Katharine Drexel's intercession was sought in an effort to establish a preexisting history of devotion and seeking out a singular saint.

In such a case as this, where does the process go from here? Passing the review of the medical bureau as being without natural explanation, the report of a cure is passed on to the board of nine theological reviewers, who examine the details of the requested intercession. After a final vote by cardinals and bishops, a recommendation to recognize the miracle will then be passed on to the pope. He will then issue an order for the Congregation for the Causes of Saints to promulgate a decree recognizing the miracle in question that thereby will lead to the beatification or canonization of that individual. A further subsequent consistory with resident and visiting cardinals in Rome will establish the details of the location and date of the events. The announcement of the approval of a miracle almost always leads to the speedy establishment of the beatification or canonization event, usually occurring just months in the future.

The Vatican Apostolic Archives (formerly known as the Vatican's Secret Archives) contains documentation on more than six hundred miracles pertaining to several hundred different canonization or beatifications from 1600 to the present day.[30] The records indicate that throughout the years, soon after their introduction to the medical community, new technologies were being used, implying that the best science available at the time and medical experts of that period were relied on throughout the whole history of these miracle investigations.[31] There are currently as many as two thousand open sainthood causes being considered by the Vatican.

In an effort to give just a small taste of some of these miracles the congregation has examined, here are nine that have been approved by the Vatican in American sainthood causes from 2000 to 2020. The reader is invited to examine these elsewhere in more detail if he or she wishes.

2000: Pope John Paul II approved the promulgation of a decree from the Congregation for the Causes of Saints that stated two-year-old Amy Wall was miraculously healed in 1994 of nerve deafness in both ears through the intercession of Saint Katharine Drexel (1858–1955), leading to Katharine's canonization.

2004: After receiving the unanimous affirmation from the Congregation for the Causes of Saints, Pope John Paul II approved as a miracle a 1992

medical cure that involved Kate Mahoney, a
fourteen-year-old New York girl who recovered
from multiple organ failure after friends and
family prayed with a relic for the intercession of
Saint Marianne Cope (1838–1918).

2006:   Pope Benedict XVI approved the promulgation
of the decree that a miraculous cure had taken
place when an Indiana man named Phil McCord
had his failing eyesight restored through the intercession of Saint Théodore Guérin (1798–1856).

2008:   The miraculous recovery in 1999 through the
intercession of Saint Damien of Molokai (1840–
1889) of Audrey Toguchi, a Hawaiian woman
with metastasized liposarcoma, a terminal cancer that arises in fat cells, was approved by Pope
Benedict XVI.

2011:   Pope Benedict signed and approved the prom-
ulgation of the decree of a miracle received by
Sharon Smith, a sixty-five-year-old woman from
Chittenango, New York, who was healed from
pancreatitis in 2005 through the intercession of
Saint Marianne Cope (1838–1918).

2011:   Pope Benedict XVI approved the second miracle
needed for the canonization of Kateri Tekakwitha
(1656–1680) when Jake Finkbonner, a young
boy in Washington State, survived a severe flesh-
eating bacterium in 2006.

2013:   The miraculous restoration of vision in 1963 to an
eight-year-old boy, Michael Mencer, who had gone
legally blind because of macular degeneration was

attributed to Blessed Miriam Teresa Demjanovich (1901–1927) and validated by Pope Francis.

2017:   Pope Francis approved a 2012 miracle through the intercession of Blessed Solanus Casey: the cure of Paula Medina Zarate of Panama from ichthyosis, a genetic skin condition.

2020:   Fr. Michael McGivney, the founder of the Knights of Columbus, was declared venerable after Rome approved the miraculous cure of an unborn child named Michael Schachle from fetal hydrops, a fatal condition of fluid buildup around the vital organs.

The International Lourdes Medical Committee (Comité Médical International de Lourdes)

Outside of Rome, the only place in the entire world with a well-established medical commission for investigating miraculous cures can be found in Lourdes, France, the site of the 1858 Marian apparitions to fourteen-year-old Saint Bernadette Soubirous. At the Virgin Mary's request in the third apparition, this little girl got down on her knees to dig in the soil, revealing a spring of water which would go on to heal, almost immediately, a woman with a disabled arm and a blind man, both of whom washed in the water. When so many more began posting notices of cures received in the waters, it became necessary to set up formal medical examinations to separate the true healings from the hoaxes, thus preventing false claims from tarnishing the image of the shrine or the Catholic Church at large.

Each year, as many as six million pilgrims visit the shrine in Lourdes, including eighty thousand *malades* (the French word used at Lourdes for ill or sick persons). Almost eight thousand reports of "remarkable" cures have been received and considered by the Bureau des Constatations Médicales, with seventy of those determined by the International Lourdes Medical Committee (CMIL) to be without scientific explanation, and later went on to be formally declared miracles by the local bishop. Of those, seventy have been declared to be without scientific explanation and are considered to be official miracles.

Lourdes is not the only shrine where miracles of healing have been reported, even if involvement and public pronouncements by the Vatican are few and far between. The Shrine of Our Lady of Knock in September 2019 made one of these rare announcements regarding the 1989 healing of a pilgrim named Marion Carroll from a severe case of multiple sclerosis, with the disappearance of the characteristic brain and spinal scarring verified by MRI scans. The National Shrine of Our Lady of Good Help in Champion, Wisconsin—the site of the only church-approved Marian apparitions in the United States—has had reports of numerous physical, mental, and spiritual healings. In response, the Champion shrine begun plans to establish their own medical bureau after the Lourdes model.

What is that model? When a case is submitted to the Medical Bureau, sometimes by interested doctors on pilgrimage, up to 250 doctors throughout the lifetime of the case may pour over the records, and examinations of the patient will continue for three years or more. If the cure stands up to this scrutiny, the case is passed on to the international medical committee of twenty medical experts who meet annually to decide such matters. Specialists in the condition will follow up on the patient, pursuing further tests, and reevaluating the results. They then present the case to their peers for a vote.

Interestingly, the number of approved cases at Lourdes in recent years has seen a decline: there have only been six miracles declared in the last six decades. The reasons are probably obvious. Modern medications for infectious diseases have taken care of many would-be visitors to Lourdes, and there were likely "miraculous cures" from past decades that nowadays could have a simple scientific explanation. Psychiatric conditions are also excluded now since those diagnoses lack certainty, and the proof of recovery is difficult to ascertain.

The fact is, our scientific understanding of the molecular basis of diseases has grown tremendously in recent decades, resulting in fewer conditions being medically unexplainable, so the challenge for finding miraculous cures at Lourdes is increasing. And with various new technologies available for assessment with many laboratory tests and clinical examinations to consider, the time for evaluation of a potential Lourdes miracle is extended more than ever.

Considering everything we know in the medical community now, it makes those six miracles in recent times all the more phenomenal. Discrediting a few miracles from yesterday does not discredit authentic miracles of today. Better instruments help add strength to these medical evaluations: they clearly distinguish those results that are explainable phenomena from those that are truly inexplicable. Superior diagnostic tools in use worldwide also help to prevent misdiagnosis, which may still be the largest challenge faced by the CMIL. A person's condition may have improved after a visit to Lourdes, but if the initial diagnosis was wrong from the outset, it makes the before-and-after comparison very difficult.

One of the most recent miracles at Lourdes involved the healing of a French nun, Sister Bernadette Moriau of the Franciscan Oblate Sisters of the Sacred Heart of Jesus, from cauda equina syndrome.

In 1966, at the age of twenty-seven, Sister Bernadette began suffering from lower back pain, which lead to four failed operations and other treatments. Less than a decade later, her condition had progressed such that she needed to abandon her work as a nurse, and over time, she became incapable of walking long distances. She later began suffering from sphincter disfunction. Some minimally effective treatments were applied: a spinal neurostimulator in 1992, a rigid, cervical-lumbar corset in 1999, and a splint in 2005 to help with her left foot, which had developed an equinus contracture. Sister Bernadette had begun to take morphine in 1994 to help with the extreme pain

But in 2008, she participated in her diocesan pilgrimage to Lourdes. On July 11, she experienced a feeling of calm and warmth spreading throughout her body, and she was inspired to get rid of all her medical aids. Her foot—now mobile—had returned to a normal position, and her sphincter disorders were gone. She immediately stopped taking all her pain medication and using the spinal neurostimulator. Remarkably, she was able to walk five kilometers the next day in celebration of her sudden cure.

Recipients of potential miracles at Lourdes like Sister Bernadette must present themselves and revisit Lourdes over the course of many years, coming before the medical bureau to answer questions and be examined. Sister Bernadette was examined in Lourdes in 2009, 2013, and 2016, which prompted the medical commission to determine that her healing was sudden, instantaneous, complete, and lasting. They declared at their 2016 annual meeting that it was "an unexplained healing, within our current limits of scientific knowledge."[32] The bishops of Tarbes and Lourdes, copresidents of the CMIL, then sent a letter to the bishop of Beauvais, Benoît-Gonnin, who, after meeting with the diocesan commission, announced the miracle in a letter dated February 11, 2018, the feast of Our Lady of Lourdes. Bishop Benoît-Gonnin declared the "prodigious-miraculous" character of Sister Bernadette's healing, adding, "This healing reaffirms for us the loving and active presence of Our Lady in the lives of the faithful who, like her, want to be open to the Word of God and to put it into practice."[33]

The Perseverance of Prayer

The centuries-old practice of verifying sainthood through miracles becomes more challenging with the passing of time and the advancing of science. As knowledge of the human body grows, less phenomena will be deemed unexplainable, and the processes of the body will be pointed to as the causes for recoveries. Some past healings once considered miraculous may be seen in a new light. In addition, as technology continues to advance, fewer diseases will require miraculous cures. We simply don't need to pray for a miracle if an antibiotic or a surgery will heal us. Some conditions that were considered fatal just decades ago are now treatable with routine drugs and surgery. For example, some patients suffering from strokes, multiple sclerosis, and traumatic brain and spinal cord injuries are able to walk with devices that stimulate the peroneal nerve with electrical pulses, or by taking drugs billed as "the walking pill."[34] Still more, cochlear implants allow the deaf to hear, and retinal transplants can restore sight to the blind.

Those of us who believe in miracles and are people of faith should not be bitter about these medical advances just because they may undermine claims of the miraculous. Clearly, they are a gift, both from God and from the hard-working men and women who develop them. In a way, they are a "miracle" of a different sort. Still more, these advances can help verify with even more precision and accuracy the authenticity of a miraculous healing. So let us praise God for them and not see them as an enemy to our faith.

And let us not forget also that any of us who have ever sat beside the hospital bed of a family member and were plagued by helplessness, grief, and anxiety, know that our reliance on prayer will never fade. No matter how effective medical advances become, they will *never* conquer all of the maladies and conditions of the human body. In other words, they will never fully eradicate our dependence on God. The power of prayer will persevere until the end of all the ages; therefore, let us persevere in our prayer and always have the faith that a miracle is possible. Let us continue to look to heaven when desperation overwhelms us. Let us ask for the intercession of the saints, and the saints-in-waiting, to cure us and our family members by taking our petitions to God.

5

Incorruptibles

The Veneration of Relics

The word *relic* means "a fragment," or some remnant of an object from the past. Though there can be secular relics, such as old bullets from World War I-era guns, generally the term is reserved for sacred objects, physical things that have a direct association with the saints or Christ himself.

But not all relics are created equal. They run the gamut from the mundane—tiny patches of clothing and everyday possessions—to the spectacular—the annual liquefying blood of Saint Januarius or pieces of the true cross. These distinctions break up relics into three classes: first-class, second-class, and third-class.

A first-class relic is from the actual body of a saint. Typically, it is a small bone fragment contained in an ossuary for safekeeping and display. Parts of Saint Catherine of Siena's body are scattered all throughout Italy, and Saint Teresa of Ávila's heart is approached by many pilgrims in Spain. In recent times, the blood of Pope Saint John Paul II was on display in a reliquary for the faithful to see at his beatification in 2012. These are all examples of first-class relics.

Second-class relics include a saint's personal effects, those things that he or she touched and interacted with. A swath of fabric from the saint's clothing or a small possession, such as a rosary, are examples of second-class relics.

Finally, a third-class relic is something that has physically touched a first- or second-class relic. While these are not as "intimate" as first- and second-class relics, they allow more people to come in contact with these sacred objects. First- and second-class relics are usually kept in one secure place for safekeeping, while third-class relics can be more widely distributed (though some first- and second-class relics are brought on tours around the world so the faithful can venerate them).

As with many Catholic practices, the veneration of relics has become widely misunderstood. It is seen by non-Catholics as blasphemous, even macabre. But neither of these accusations are true. These sacred objects are given no worship; rather, they are sought out to pay homage to God and the holy men and women who served him best in this life.

Usually, the faithful seek out relics to ask for a miracle, or more specifically, for a miracle of healing. The skeptics should know that this practice has biblical roots. When a dead man was touched to the bones of the prophet Elisha, he immediately came back to life (see 2 Kgs 13:20–21). In Matthew's Gospel, we read about the woman with a hemorrhage being healed simply by touching the hem of Jesus's cloak (see Mt 9:20–22). And finally, the book of Acts shows us that Paul's handkerchiefs were second-class relics imbued with God's saving power: "And God did extraordinary miracles by the hands of Paul, so that handkerchiefs or aprons were carried away from his body to the sick, and diseases left them and the evil spirits came out of them" (Acts 19:11–12).

Similar acts of healing came to those who were simply "touched" by Saint Peter's shadow (see Acts 5:12–15).

But these are stories from Scripture, stories from so long ago, from the time of Christ and even before. Such miracles cannot still occur through the mysterious power of relics any longer, can they?

As it turns out, in the tradition of the Church, there is a long history extending even into today's time that shows the veneration of relics can bring about miraculous healings and, more importantly, buttresses the faith of people all over the world.

Two remarkable modern healings from blindness in America involved people praying with the relics of saints. In 2013, Pope Francis approved a miracle of the restoration of perfect vision to an eight-year-old boy, Michael Mencer, who had gone legally blind because of macular degeneration. He and his family prayed to Blessed Miriam Teresa Demjanovich (1901–1927) with a memento containing a strand of her hair. In October 2015, Dafne Gutierrez, a thirty-year-old mother of three children who had lost her eyesight to Arnold-Chiari malformation had her eyesight restored after venerating a relic of Saint Charbel (1828–1898) in Phoenix, Arizona.[35]

These are just two of many instances where relics have been shown to bring about a miraculous cure.

Understanding Incorruptibles

In the spectrum of relics, the incorruptible bodies of the saints, which defy the natural decay found in the laws of nature, are arguably among the most phenomenal spectacles of the Catholic faith.

Sometimes, no matter how poorly they were buried—in a flimsy coffin or none at all and in different climates in different parts of the world—the bodies of a small percentage of saints remain in a protected state. These "incorruptibles" look remarkably similar to how they did when they died, with finer details like skin, hair, eyelashes, and fingernails perfectly preserved, and muscles still soft and flexible. Typically, with this lack of decay, the bodies do not possess the stench of death, and some are even graced with sweet-smelling fragrances, like that of roses. Still more, some incorruptibles exude fragrant oil or blood years after their burial.

Approximately half of all the known incorruptibles are found in Italy. The rest are scattered around the world—in Ecuador, France, Spain, Poland, Austria, Belgium, Germany, India, Peru, and Lebanon.[36] The disproportionate amount found in Italy presumably stems from the Church being headquartered in Rome, leading to more study of the phenomenon and more bodies being exhumed. It is possible, even likely, that plenty of other incorruptibles are yet to be discovered in other parts of the world.

First seen in the body of the second-century Roman martyr Saint Cecilia, incorruption is a gift generally claimed by Catholics alone, partly because it is an element of the tradition of the Church to venerate (and obtain) relics and to inspect the corpses prior to beatifications, canonizations, and transfers of burial locations. Other than the Orthodox Churches, most other religions do not have these practices. There is an overwhelming sense of respect—at times fascination—in Catholic tradition with the body of a holy person that is not found in other faiths.

Despite the eye-popping nature of this strange phenomenon, the simple fact is that there is more to understanding incorruptibility than first meets the eye. There are certain distinctions that should be acknowledged in order to preserve the integrity of authentic miracles.

Throughout the world and its many cultures, preserved corpses exist due to three distinct possibilities: deliberate preservation, accidental preservation, and incorruptibility.[37] There are of course examples of bodies fighting off decay after death outside the Church, but these usually fall within the first two categories. We might think of the Egyptian mummies or other mummies found in Peru (Incans), Babylon, and Tibet, which were deliberately preserved. And other corpses that are at rest in perfect atmospheric conditions may be accidentally protected.[38] These mummies do not usually appear as well preserved—often dried out, brittle, and discolored—as the flexible body of a saint who has been spared the ravages of time by God without the need for an advanced preservation process or ideal temperatures.

Take, for example, Saint Francis Xavier (1506–1552), missionary to the Far East and cofounder of the Society of Jesus, who remained in a state of perfect preservation for 142 years. The body of the Spanish mystic and poet Saint John of the Cross (1542–1591) remains flexible to this very day.[39]

But even within the classification of incorruptibles, there are distinctions and different levels of preservation, as well as practices within the Church surrounding these bodies.

For one, it is not uncommon for only part of a saint's body to remain incorrupt, while the rest of it decomposes naturally. We can see this "partial incorruptibility" in Saint Pio of Pietrelcina (1887–1968) and Saint John Vianney (1786–1859), whose hearts have been identified as incorrupt and have gone on worldwide tours for the Catholic faithful to see, while the rest of their corpses are *not* in a state of unnatural preservation. In the case of Saint Anthony of Padua (1195–1231), his body decomposed normally, but the remains of his tongue, larynx, and jaw are well preserved in his basilica in the city of his death. (These items are venerated and held in esteem as a tribute to his unique powers of preaching!)

Other saints have been found to be incorrupt at the time they are exhumed, only to later decay. In some cases, after the tombs were unsealed, exposure to microbes and contaminants from the environment led to rapid decomposition.[40] In other cases, in an effort to study a body or transfer it from one location to the next (for beatification or canonization ceremonies), the body can begin to degrade in appearance.

Due to these challenges, the Church has taken steps to help preserve the incorrupt bodies of some saints, including the use of modern embalming techniques, or by waxing over the bodies to preserve the features of a formerly incorrupt corpse.

But there is no attempt to hide these efforts or pass them off as miraculous. Just because a body is treated today to maintain its preservation in no way belittles the miracle that it remained preserved, in some cases for hundreds of years, in a coffin below the earth, long before embalming methods were commonplace. And while partial incorruptibility may not be as wonderous as complete incorruptibility, it is still a wonder indeed that a saint's heart or some other organ would fail to decompose. The Church does not try to speculate on why things may end up this way but rather sees it as a miracle all the same, which it can hold up to aid the faith of its members.

Throughout history, the bodies of over one hundred saints (or approximately 1 percent of the estimated ten thousand saints in Catholic Church history) have been identified as being in a state of extraordinary preservation for at least some time. But it may surprise some to learn that the Church does not consider incorruptibility to be a guarantee of holiness and no longer gives official recognition of preservations as it once did through the Congregation of Rites. Prospero Lambertini, the future Pope Benedict XIV, who, as we have noted, formulated the criteria for medical miracles still in use by the Church today, paid special attention to this phenomenon in his work *De Cadaverum Incorruptione*, in which he addressed the incorrupt bodies of some saints. He insisted that their corpses needed to be in a near perfect state of preservation over the course of many years for it to be worthy of being considered a canonization miracle. A rare case of incorruption used for establishing sainthood is Saint Andrew Bobola, whose corpse endured rough handling during several relocations and still remained perfectly fresh for more than three hundred years.

Despite the fact that the Catholic Church no longer considers incorruptibility as a proof for holiness and therefore will not officially examine cases, some scientific study has been done in the past on purported incorruptibles. Let us examine some of those now, with a special focus placed on the exhumation of Saint Bernadette.

The Exhumation of Saint Bernadette Soubirous

One of the most famous, well-documented, and best preservations of an incorruptible body is that of Saint Bernadette Soubirous, who died on April 16, 1879.

In the Rite of Recognition, the corpse is exhumed and examined as a part of the canonization process that verifies the remains of the deceased and allows relics to be retrieved. The first "Identification of the Body" performed on Bernadette occurred on September 22, 1909, thirty years after her death, with Monsignor Gauthey, bishop of Nevers, the church tribunal, three witnesses (Abbe Perreau, the mother superior of the order, Marie-Josephine Forestier, and her deputy), the doctors (Doctors A. Jourdan and Ch. David), the stonemasons, and the carpenters all present. They entered the chapel together and swore an oath to tell the truth and fulfilled the other requisite legal formalities.

After the stone had been lifted, the wooden coffin was unscrewed and the lead coffin was cut open. Bernadette's body was found to be in a state of perfect preservation and was free of any putrid odor.

From the report:

The coffin was opened in the presence of the Bishop of Nevers, the mayor of the town, his principal deputy, several canons and ourselves. We noticed no smell. The body was clothed in the habit of Bernadette's order. The habit was damp. Only the face, hands and forearms were uncovered.

The head was tilted to the left. The face was dull white. The skin clung to the muscles and the muscles adhered to the bones. The sockets of the eyes were covered by the eye-lids. The brows were flat on the skin and stuck to the arches above the eyes. The lashes of the right eyelid were stuck to the skin. The nose was dilated and shrunken. The mouth was open slightly and it could be seen that the teeth were still in place. The hands, which were crossed on her breast, were perfectly preserved, as were the nails. The hands still held a rusting rosary. The veins on the forearms stood out.

Like the hands, the feet were wizened and the toe-nails were still intact (one of them was torn off when the corpse was washed). When the habits had been removed and the veil lifted from the head, the whole of the shriveled body could be seen, rigid and taut in every limb.

It was found that the hair, which had been cut short, was stuck to the head and still attached to the skull—that the ears were in a state of perfect preservation—that the left side of the body was slightly higher than the right from the hip up.

The stomach had caved in and was taut like the rest of the body. It sounded like cardboard when struck.

The left knee was not as large as the right. The ribs protruded as did the muscles in the limbs.

So rigid was the body that it could be rolled over and back for washing.

The lower parts of the body had turned slightly black. This seems to have been the result of the carbon of which quite large quantities were found in the coffin.

In witness of which we have duly drawn up this present statement in which all is truthfully recorded.

Nevers, September 22, 1909

-Drs. Ch. David, A. Jourdan.[41]

It is fascinating to read such a report to see the detail with which the examiners took and to be there in the moment with them when they exhumed this holy saint whom the Mother of God appeared to in 1858.

Various conditions—type of soil, temperature, humidity in the chapel vault—can be more conducive to a corpse being preserved in a remarkable way. In the case of Bernadette, however, her habit was found to be damp, the rosary rusted, and the crucifix had turned green, all pointing to conditions unlikely to preserve flesh. Yet she did not look how a thirty-year-old corpse should look (or smell).

Before the body was washed and laid in a new coffin, within the few hours in which it had been exposed to the air, the body had started turning black. After the coffin was closed, it was soldered, screwed down, and sealed with seven seals.[42]

A second "Identification of the Body" occurred on August 13, 1913, after her cause for beatification and canonization was officially opened. Doctor Talon and Doctor Comte did the examination in the presence of the bishop of Nevers, the police commissioner, representatives of the municipalities, and members of the church tribunal. The same proceedings of exhumation took place in accordance with canon and civil law, but this time, the doctors examined the body and wrote their own independent personal reports.

All details were consistent between the doctors with the previous examination several years earlier, except for the of appearance of "patches of mildew and a layer of salt which seems to be calcium salt."

Doctor Comte reported, "When the coffin was opened the body appeared to be absolutely intact and odourless. (Dr. Talon was more specific: 'There was no smell of putrefaction and none of those present experienced any discomfort.') The body is practically mummified, covered with patches of mildew and quite a notable layer of salts which appear to be calcium salts. The skeleton is complete, and it was possible to carry the body to a table without any trouble. The skin has disappeared in some places, but it is still present on most parts of the body. Some of the veins are still visible."[43]

Pope Pius X made a pronouncement affirming Bernadette's virtues and declared her venerable, thus opening her path to beatification. In order for that next step to occur, her body needed to be identified a third time during a new exhumation, which would also serve the purpose of acquiring relics for Rome, Lourdes, and her order.

Doctor Comte also details some of the excisions he made:

At the request of the Bishop of Nevers I detached and removed the rear section of the fifth and sixth right ribs as relics; I noted that there was a resistant, hard mass in the thorax, which was the liver covered by the diaphragm. I also took a piece of the diaphragm and the liver beneath it as relics, and can affirm that this organ was in a remarkable state of preservation. I also removed the two patella bones to which the skin clung and which were covered with more clinging calcium matter.

Finally, I removed the muscle fragments right and left from the outsides of the thighs. These muscles were also in a very good state of preservation and did not seem to have putrefied at all.[44]

Doctor Comte concludes, "From this examination I conclude that the body of the Venerable Bernadette is intact, the skeleton is complete, the muscles have atrophied, but are well preserved; only the skin, which has shriveled, seems to have suffered from the effects of the damp in the coffin."[45]

Thus, the medical reports on the three exhumations, in the presence each time of the civil and church authorities, contain sworn testimonies verifying that it is truly Bernadette's body and she is remarkably intact with no embalming and with only a few relics removed.

Pope Pius XI officially beatified Bernadette on June 14, 1925. For her placement in her shrine, the nuns dressed Bernadette's body in a new habit and light wax masks, which had previously been made from imprints of her face and hands by a sculptor. But her body remains incorrupt, and millions of pilgrims have gone to the Chapel of Saint Gidard in Nevers, France to venerate her relics.

The Authenticity of Incorruptibles

While incorruptibility is not considered to be a miracle used for sainthood causes, and the attention given to Saint Bernadette is not typical for more modern sainthood causes, there has been an attempt by the Vatican to understand the reality of these preservations from centuries ago.

According to Joan Carroll Cruz in her definitive book on the topic, *The Incorruptibles: A Study of the Incorruption of the Bodies of Various Catholic Saints and Beati*, "The incorruptibles, for the most part, were never embalmed or treated in any manner."[46]

Many corpses remain magnificently intact despite the various attempts to check the body, redress it with fresh vestments, or transfer it to new burial locations. Oftentimes, due to poverty, conditions, and poor burial materials and practices, bodies are not protected from excessive moisture or other factors that would hasten the decomposition process. Despite all that, Christian history is filled with stories of incorruptible saints.

In more recent decades, after the publication of Cruz's guide to the incorruptibles, more information has come to light related to the traditional practices of embalming and preserving the saints.

Starting in the mid-1980s, at the Vatican's request, Italian pathologists, chemists, and radiologists have examined the bodies of more than two dozen preserved saints and beati with the conclusion that they were incontrovertibly mummified (deliberate preservation), while others were protected from decay by favorable environmental conditions (accidental preservation), such as lying in tombs lined with alkaline stone or at temperatures below 60° Fahrenheit, the threshold most favorable to bacterial growth.[47]

Ezio Fulcheri, a pathologist at the University of Genoa, found that Saint Margaret of Cortona had been artificially mummified. Long incisions along her sides, clues of the application of chemicals and techniques to preserve her internal organs, were clearly made after death and had been sewn shut with a coarse black thread. Several other mystics— Saint Clare of Montefalco, Blessed Margaret of Metola, Saint Catherine of Siena, Saint Bernardine of Siena, and Saint Rita of Cascia—were found to be similarly mummified.[48]

So then is the phenomenon of incorruptibility a fraud? Is it a trick the Catholic Church plays on the faithful to keep them kneeling in the pews (and dropping their money in the collection plate)?

Not quite.

Some saints, after rigorous tests and examinations, were scientifically proven to have no special conditions in their final resting place, nor any preparation to preserve them after burial. For example, pathologist Gino Fornaciari and a team of scientists from the University of Pisa examined Saint Zita with an intra-body camera and found no sign of post-mortem cuts or methods of preservation. Other saints—such as Saint Ubald of Gubbio, Blessed Margaret of Savoy, and Saint Savina Petrilli—were also scientifically verified as being inexplicably preserved.[49]

Despite doubts which arise concerning the veracity of incorruptibility claims, the phenomenon still does not have a satisfactory scientific explanation in *all* cases. Even if a good portion of the preservations are attributable to specialized mummification techniques or unintentional conditions favorable to preservation, other corpses which have received no special burial and have endured transfers between several different locations have survived for many years in an unusual and surprising state of perfection. Other corpses that have been exposed to environments which would have facilitated their decomposition have inexplicably survived the test of time.

There is an expression: "the exception proves the rule." It refers to a stereotypical understanding that is seemingly debunked by one case manifesting an opposite conclusion. The "exception" to the stereotype or the common expectation "proves the rule" because we are all so surprised that it does not follow the common and expected outcome. Rather than exposing a lie or disproving something, it actually highlights the truth of the claim by shining a light on all the other evidence that supports the thesis.

Might we coin another expression in regards to our incorruptibles? "The science proves the miracle." This is a point we have highlighted before but we will do so again here.

If modern science can show that some incorruptibles were *intentionally* preserved, or were simply kept in natural conditions favorable to preservation, this does not undermine the miraculous claims of the phenomenon altogether *but rather proves the miraculous all the more* in the cases where science cannot give an explanation. The Church is perfectly willing—in fact, will be the first to acknowledge—when science holds claim to an explanation of an unusual occurrence. As Catholics, we do not try to claim a miracle when one is not there. But when science cannot offer an explanation, we are ready to fall on our knees and thank God for a miracle.

6

Apparitions

Verifying Visions and Locutions

Every man, woman, and child who has claimed to see a mystical vision is first met with skepticism, even from good priests, bishops, and their own parents. Lúcia of Fatima was scolded by her mother, who accused her of lying about seeing the Virgin Mary, and her parish priest wondered if she was having demonic visions!

As outsiders looking back on the situation, it is easy to think how cruel these accusations were. "Why wouldn't they believe this sweet, saintly child?" we ask ourselves. Of course, we have the benefit of hindsight's perfect vision. We should be slow to judge skeptics who, at the time, were not privy to the full story that unfolded in *their future* and *our past*. Just imagine if your own child or niece or nephew came to you and told you they were seeing the Virgin Mary floating in a tree in your backyard. Would you believe? Additionally, there have been plenty of cases of fraudulent claims over the years, giving credence to any doubt skeptics may have.

Unlike other types of alleged miracles, like weeping statues and Eucharistic miracles, that can be verified or at least studied with scientific test results, claims of seeing visions or hearing locutions have no such evidence. Instead, these phenomena are most typically examined by a careful review of the history, character, and mental health of the seer or group of seers. An approval or denial by ecclesial investigators typically rests on the impeccable character of those claiming to see the visions, on the testimony of reliable witnesses, or—on very rare occasions—on other "signs" that may accompany the visions, such as Juan Diego's *tilma*, the miracle of the sun at Fatima, or the miraculous spring of water in Lourdes. The only "experiments" one might see performed by doctors is while a seer appears to be in ecstasy to test the authenticity of their rapture. But, of course, for this to happen, doctors must be present at the time of the apparition, which isn't always possible.

While we tend to focus on all the approved apparitions that have occurred throughout history (and as well we should), there have been plenty of frauds and cases of mental sickness. According to the Vatican guidelines for the judgment of apparition claims found in the 1978 *Normae Congregationis de Modo Procedendi in Diudicandis Praesumptis Apparitionibus ac Revelationibus* ("Norms of the Congregation for Proceeding in Judging Alleged Apparitions and Revelations"), an alleged vision can be negatively judged as *constat de non supernaturalitate* ("Established as not supernatural") when any of the following factors are present:

*Saint Bernadette Soubirous' Crystal Coffin, Nevers, France.
Godong / Bridgeman Images*

One of history's most remarkable cases of incorruption is in Nevers, France where rests the body of St. Bernadette Soubirous, famed for her eighteen visions of Our Lady of Lourdes in 1858.

The festival of San Gennaro, Naples Italy, Adam Eastland / Alamy Stock Photo

Every year on September 19, the Feast of San Gennaro, the dried blood of St. Januarius, the third century bishop and martyr, liquefies in the presence of the bishop and thousands of gathered faithful. The miracle is seen as a portent of a promising year for the city. On the rare occasions where this phenomenon has not occurred, the city has reported volcanic eruptions, earthquakes, plagues and other calamities.

Saint Januarius, Michelangelo Merisi da Caravaggio, Louis Finson, Public domain, via Wikimedia Commons

La Grotte des Apparition, Lourdes France, Godong/UIG / Bridgeman Images

The Medical Bureau of Lourdes has investigated thousands of reported miraculous healings from which it has recognized seventy cures as having passed the Church's strict "Lambertini Criteria," declaring they are without natural explanation.

Virgin de Las Lajas, Desconocido del siglo XVIII, Public domain, via Wikimedia Commons

Ipiales, Colombia was the site of the 1754 vision of the Blessed Virgin Mary to Maria Meneses de Quiñones and her deaf-mute daughter, Rosa, as they ran into a cave to escape a rainstorm. Rosa was cured of her ailments, and still today there is a miraculous image colored into the stone, that is venerated by pilgrims from all over the world.

On May 13, 1917—the sixth and final apparition of the Virgin Mary to Lucia dos Santos and her cousins, Jacinta and Francisco Marto, the shepherd children of Fatima—a crowd of 70,0000 witnesses gathered at the Cova da Iria in the rain and mud to see a promised miracle. Believers and atheists alike reported the sun dancing and giving off colors before plummeting to the earth, with the suddenly dry earth ruling out a case of mass hysteria.

1917 Newspaper, Fatima, Portugal, Alvenido de Almedia, journalist a the O Seculo dialy, Public domain, via Wikimedia Commons

(Opposite) Lúcia Santos, Jacinta and Francisco Marto, 1917 Fatima, Portugal, Attributed to Joshua Benoliel, Public domain, via Wikimedia Commons

Judah Ruah, photograph for the news paper O Seculo, published the 1917-09-29 on the news paper Illustracao Portugueza, Public domain, via Wikimedia Commons

The 1531 acheiropoietos (Greek: "not made from human hands") image of the Virgen de Guadalupe on the tilma of St. Juan Diego is Mexico's most enduring religious symbol, it is visited by twenty million pilgrims a year who come to venerate the image at the Basilica. The image is the only existing codex from that era on agave fibre in such well-preserved condition.

Basilica of Our Lady of Guadalupe, Mexico, part of Wiki Loves Pyramids. Photograph by Mike Peel (www.mikepeel.net)., CC BY-SA 4.0 via Wikimedia Commons

An alleged photo of the Virgin Mary above the Church of Virgin Mary in Zeitoun, Cairo, via Wikimedia Commons

From 1968 to 1971, the Virgin Mary was reported to be seen walking, while surrounded by lights and doves, on the rooftop of St. Mark's Coptic Orthodox church in Zeitoun, Egypt. This was witnessed by thousands, including Christians, Jews, and Muslims.

On January 17, 1797, an inexplicable image of the Virgin Mary was discovered to appear on the window of Rosina Buecher in Absam, Austria, as she awaited the return home of her father from a mining accident. The image returned after the glass was cleaned and was recognized as authentic by the local bishop.

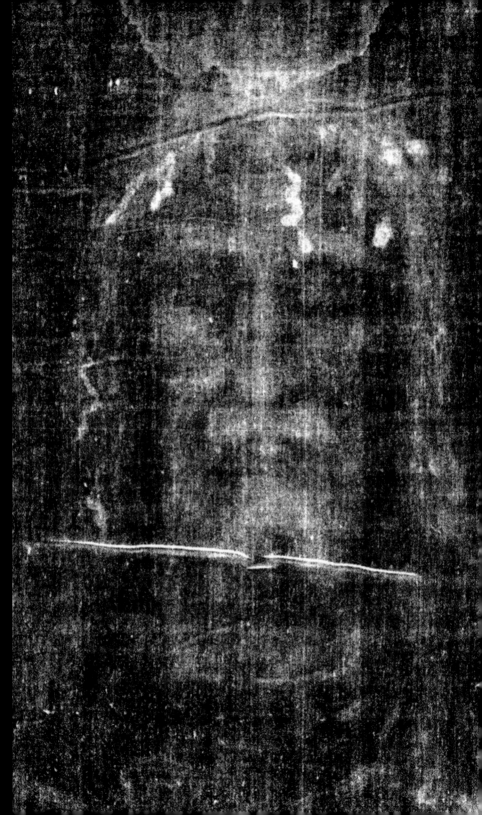

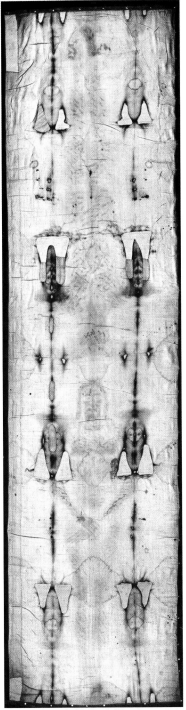

The Shroud of Turin, the human blood-stained purported burial cloth of Christ, which resides in Turin, Italy, bears an image that has been examined by scientists over the centuries, still without a definitive conclusion being drawn on how it was made. Questions persist about its origins despite 1988 carbon testing which placed it in the Middle Ages.

(Opposite) Secondo Pia's 1898 negative of the image on the Shroud of Turin, Universal History Archive/UIG / Bridgeman Images

Full-length photograph of the Shroud of Turin, Giuseppe Enrie, 1931, Public domain, via Wikimedia Commons

Holy Shroud of Turin : Christ face, 1994, Farabola / Bridgeman Images

Photo, Michael O'Neill

In the summer of 2018, a bronze statue of Our Lady of Guadalupe at the Our Lady of Guadalupe parish in Hobbs, New Mexico, began to weep tears. All told, the statue was said to have wept on four separate occasions, enough that the local diocese of Las Cruces initiated an investigation. The local bishop, Oscar Cantú, released an official statement in 2019 declaring the tears naturally inexplicable, saying, "We have not discerned natural causes for the statue's emitting of liquid."

Miracolo Eucaristico di Lanciano, Junior, Public domain, via Wikimedia Commons

Around the year 750, a Basilian monk with doubts about the Real Presence encountered what is considered by many to be the first known Eucharistic miracle when the Consecrated Host began to manifest true flesh and true blood, a reality that has been investigated by scientists over the centuries. Other such occurrences have been documented on rare occasions in locations all over the world.

Throughout his life, St. Pio of Pietrelcina (1887–1968), popularly known as "Padre Pio," was a Capuchin friar reported to exhibit various mystical phenomena, including bilocation, reading of souls in the confessional, healing of the sick, and—for fifty years—bearing the wounds of Christ, known as the stigmata.

Francesco Forgione, called Padre Pio de Pietrelcina (1887-1968), Photo 1959 / Bridgeman Images

1. Glaring errors in facts
2. Doctrinal errors attributed to God or Mary
3. Pursuit of financial gain
4. Gravely immoral acts committed by the visionary
5. Psychological disorders or tendencies in the visionary

Personality tests like the Minnesota Multiphasic Personality Inventory may be administered by a psychologist to ferret out any mental health issues. Special attention is also given to assessing the subject's ability to exhibit a healthy and deep spiritual life integration. Strong relationships with others and a faith life acting as an anchoring force are considered positive markers, while an unhealthy spirituality can be identified by chaos, rigidity, and a lack of inner peace.

One of the earliest scientific tests ever administered to a Marian visionary was at Lourdes, when in 1858 fourteen-year-old Saint Bernadette famously reported seeing eighteen visions of the Virgin Mary. On February 20, 1858, Dr. Pierre-Romaine Dozous, a well-known local physician, evaluated Bernadette and declared that there was no indication of "nervous excitement" (meaning there was nothing that would suggest her supposed visions stemmed from a psychological condition). On April 7, 1858, he observed her putting her hand through the flame of a candle without feeling pain or getting burned during her ecstasy. Several witnesses also testified to her reverence and total absorption while she was at the grotto. Finally, despite the fact that she was repeatedly questioned and cross-examined, her testimony never wavered or showed any signs of inconsistency.

Similar tests were administered during the later Church-approved apparitions at Beauring, Belgium. While the visionaries were in the midst of ecstasy, doctors performed stimulus tests to pinch, slap, and prick the children and shine flashlights in their eyes. There was no response from the children during the apparition. One doctor even put visionary Gilberte Voisin's left hand in a flame, but there was no physical reaction or sign of injury.

In general, Marian apparitions are typically not subjected to scientific analysis beyond basic physical tests or psychoanalysis like this. Only a few cases in modern history have seen enough of a following that it merited scientific funding and technology to conduct a serious inquiry. Let us examine three of those stories now.

Conyers, GA (USA)

In February of 1987, Nancy Fowler of Conyers, Georgia, a middle-aged housewife and mother, began to have a long series of alleged visions of Jesus and Mary. Most of these occurred between October 13, 1990 and May 13, 1994 at a farm house, where large crowds eventually started to gather. After each alleged vision, Nancy related messages from the Blessed Mother for the United States.

When enough attention was brought to Conyers, Nancy underwent various medical and scientific tests to determine whether the visions were due to some brain abnormality, hallucinations due to disease, or psychiatric disturbance. The team leader, Ricardo Castañon, a professor of neuropsychophysiology from Bolivia, was noted for examinations of alleged supernatural events and was joined by other neurologists, EEG technicians, psychiatrists, and research and radiation scientists. Other tests were also attempted in order to gather data on atmospheric radiation changes during the apparitions. Nancy's brain activity was monitored with EEG equipment and time coordinated with a separate video recording of her behavior.

What were the results? Nancy had a normal, healthy brain. However, when she claimed to be having an apparition, the tests showed that she went into a state of 4 hertz and 3 hertz delta brain activity, which normally would be associated with deep sleep or a coma. This was despite her being fully alert.

Other tests monitored and recorded changes that occurred in the electrical conductivity of her skin. They showed a jump in readings, indicating anxiety to those reflecting normal function. Psychiatrist Doctor Hogben interviewed Nancy before the apparition and watched her during the apparition, noting "no evidence of psychotic disturbance."[50] There was no explanation or precedent given by scientists for the variations in recorded data during these tests.

Nancy Fowler had her fair share of believers and skeptics. Fowler's alleged messages, released in her three-volume book *To Bear Witness That I Am the Living Son of God*, contained many encouragements to go to Mass, receive the sacraments, and pray. They also had various problematic aspects, however, including vague predictions of future calamities, like unfulfilled seismological events and war predictions, without associated dates or times. More importantly, subjecting oneself to the authority and judgments of the Catholic Church has always been a hallmark of true mystics like Saint Pio and

Saint Faustina Kowalska, who obediently subjected themselves to the decisions of the Church. Several of the messages related by Nancy Fowler do not reflect such docility, such as Message 596 (October 6, 1992): "Jesus again spoke, 'The Church said you do not have to believe in apparitions and I say you better listen. . . . Who are you afraid of? I am leading. My Spirit speaks through you.'"

As far as how the Church judged these events, on September 19, 1991, Archbishop James P. Lyke, OFM, stated that no formal Church-sponsored investigation was necessary: "At this time, circumstances do not warrant a formal investigation into these events." Due to the lack of formal approval from the Church, he instructed that "no parish facilities may be used for the fostering of any devotion."[51]

Garabandal (Spain)

From 1961 to 1965, four young schoolgirls—Conchita González, Mari Cruz González, Jacinta González, and Mari Loli Mazón—in the rural village of San Sebastián de Garabandal (more commonly referred to as simply Garabandal) in northern Spain claimed to receive thousands of apparitions of Saint Michael the Archangel and the Virgin Mary, who allegedly imparted messages of a of a future "warning," a "miracle," and a conditional "punishment." During those years, the phenomena became internationally known and drew large crowds. The children were filmed or photographed and were subjected to psychological testing not initiated by Church authorities.

The four girls were examined by Dr. Celestino Ortiz Perez of Santander, a child psychologist and pediatrician, while they were in what was presumed to be a state of ecstasy during the apparitions. He observed:

> In this state of ecstasy they gave proof that they are beyond the explanation of medical science and all natural laws. They showed no reaction to pain, pin pricks, et cetera. Once out of their trances however, they reacted immediately. From a pediatric and psychiatric point of view, the four little girls have always been and continue to be normal. The trances in which we have observed these young girls do not fit into the framework of any psychic or any psychological pathology presently known. Our conceit falls apart when we are faced with this kind of dilemma which God bestows on us in order to point out our own medical limitations.[52]

Dr. Ricardo Puncernai, a neuropsychiatrist and director of neurological services at the university clinic in Barcelona, also examined the visionaries during their alleged ecstasies. He concluded, "Even though we try to explain only part of these extraordinary phenomena, the truth is that we do not find any natural scientific explanation which could explain the whole affair."[53]

As has been the case in other scientific examinations of Marian apparitions, independent assessments are trumped by the official investigation of the Church in order to eliminate the biases of the testing scientists and lack of control of the test conditions. A technical committee was then formed by Bishop Doroteo Fernández y Fernández, the apostolic administrator of the diocese of Santander from

1961 to 1962, consisting of three priests and professors from Santander: Fr. Juan Antonio del Val (who would later become bishop of Santander), Fr. Francisco Odriozola, and Fr. Jose María Saiz. These three were joined by two doctors, Doctor Morales, a psychiatrist from Santander, and Doctor Piñal, an anesthetist.[54]

In three visits to the site of the apparitions, the commission concluded that the events were "child's play."[55] Bishop Fernández based his conclusions on reports of this technical committee that all the events had a natural explanation. He published a statement on August 26, 1961 in which he rendered a *non constat* judgment—neither approving nor condemning the alleged apparitions: "Nothing, sufficiently presented, obliges us to affirm the supernatural nature of the events that occurred there."[56]

On November 2, 1961, just half a month after the first message of Garabandal, he released a second statement to reiterate his previous judgment: "There is no evidence that the aforementioned appearances, visions, locutions or revelations can now be sufficiently presented or taken seriously as true and authentic."[57]

Following the statements from Bishop Fernández, four consecutive bishops of Santander reaffirmed the judgment that the supernatural character of the Garabandal apparitions could not be established.[58] The official position of the Catholic Church follows the decision of this bishop and his successors: while not condemned on the basis of the content of the messages, the supernatural nature of the events could not be established. Although two of the bishop's committees declared that there were no phenomena capable of authenticating the facts as undoubtedly supernatural, they did not condemn the message. In this regard, the first commission stated, "We find nothing in need of ecclesiastical censure or condemnation, neither in the doctrine nor in the spiritual recommendations supposedly addressed to the faithful."[59] Many Marian devotees maintain an interest in these events of a half-century ago and hope for a reopening and thorough reinvestigation of the case by the diocese of Santander or by Rome.

Medjugorje (Bosnia-Herzegovina)

From the earliest days of the alleged apparitions at Medjugorje in Bosnia-Herzegovina that began on June 24, 1981, the six children who claimed to have visions and receive messages from the Virgin Mary—Ivan Dragičević, Ivanka Ivanković, Jakov Čolo, Marija Pavlović, Mirjana Dragičević, and Vicka Ivanković—were subjected to various independent medical tests from French, Italian, and Yugoslav doctors. These teams closely examined the apparitions and found no evidence of fraud or hysteria and documented no problems with the alleged visionaries. The tests included polygraphs, psychiatric tests, electrocardiogram, blood pressure and heart rhythm examinations, and electroencephalograms measuring the seers' brain waves during their purported daily ecstasies.[60]

The investigative team of Dr. Henri Joyeux, a French oncologist from the Faculty of Medicine at the University of Montpellier, examined the visionaries in June, October, and December of 1984. After all his testing, he concluded that they were not suffering from individual or collective hallucinations or hysteria. They also concluded that the visionaries were not subject to neurosis, phobias, depression, nor to cat-alepsy (lack of response to external stimuli).

Sound tests were also administered on one of the vision-aries. Ivan reacted to a sound of seventy decibels before entering his "ecstasy" but did not react to one of ninety deci-bels—equivalent to the sound of heavy traffic—which was said to demonstrate a "disconnection of the auditory path-ways during the ecstasy" of the visionary, implying that there was no reaction *during their apparitions.* Sensations travelled in a normal manner to the brain, but the findings demon-strated that the cerebral cortex did not perceive the trans-mission of the auditory and visual neuronal stimuli received from the surrounding environment.[61]

Opthalmologist Dr. Jacques Philippot claimed a slow-ing of eyelid reflexes for all the children—up to two times slower—to bright lights and that the seers' line of sight during their experience remained fixed on one point sev-eral feet above their heads, according to electro-oculographic machines. He also claimed to have measured, using initial and final electro-oculogram readings, the synchronicity of eyeball movement among the visionaries during the visions to be less than .2 seconds.

The hearts of the visionaries were also tested. Heart spe-cialist Dr. Bernard Hoarau reported that electrocardiogram, blood pressure, and heart rhythm examinations of the visionaries during their ecstasies "allow us to exclude totally the existence of dreaming, sleep, or epilepsy."[62]

Afterwards, neurologist Dr. Jean Cadhilac remarked that the testing "formally eliminates all clinical signs comparable to those observed during individual or collective hallucinations, hysteria, neurosis, or pathological ecstasy."[63]

It should be noted that the initial testing done by independent medical groups has come under fire by those who question the credentials, methodologies, and motivations of the scientists. Some have questioned the tests that have been administered themselves. For example, Professor Théophile Kammerer, president of the Lourdes International Medical Committee, remained unimpressed by the studies: "As to their level, these tests remain superficial. . . . Despite this, all the sophisticated techniques impress the simple-minded readers."[64]

Others, like prominent Medjugorje skeptic Marco Corvaglia, have pointed to the associations of the doctors conducting the studies, such as Professor Joyeux, a practicing Catholic and member of the Catholic Charismatic Renewal, having had close connections and professional collaborations and affiliations with top Medjugorje promoter and Mariologist Fr. Rene Laurentin.[65] He has also questioned the lack of instrumental testing (not simply observational testing) given the long duration of the apparitions beginning in 1981, saying, "Altogether, these tests only cover 12 presumed apparitions, each lasting just over a minute, in this period of thirty years."[66]

In the subsequent initial commission set up by the local ordinary Bishop Pavao Zanic, who publicly opposed the Medjugorje events, these independent tests were not considered; instead, he ordered his own examinations.[67] The alleged visions were given the negative judgment of *constat de non supernaturalitate* by two consecutive local bishops, until the 1991 Zadar Declaration placed the case in the wait-and-see category of *non constat de supernaturalitate* ("Not established as supernatural"). The 2010 Ruini Commission formed under Pope Benedict XVI used experts in fields like theology, Mariology, psychology, and anthropology to interview the visionaries over several years to study the messages of our Lady and fruits of the phenomenon. The results were sent to Pope Francis, who, as of 2021, has only commented informally on the report but has not rendered an official judgment. The report has since been leaked to the internet and translated in 2020,[68] showing the support of the commission (with no judgment yet from Rome) for the approval of the supernatural character of the first seven apparitions and calling for further study of the subsequent 99.9 percent of the messages, spanning more than forty years of daily and monthly alleged visits of the Virgin Mary. Instead, the pope has taken the unprecedented step of declaring this unapproved Marian site an official place of pilgrimage, assigning retired Archbishop Henryk Hoser of Poland (1942—2021) as the apostolic administrator and overseer of the shrine in order to care for the pastoral needs of pilgrims traveling there from all around the world.[69]

Allowing the Church to Render Judgment

When it comes to the scientific study of Marian apparitions, it seems that early independent tests administered without the full involvement or control of Catholic Church authorities have muddied the waters in prematurely generating the excitement and interest of the faithful. This challenges the Church's opportunity to properly handle analysis, retesting, and timing of the release of the results. On a positive note, however, these initial studies have led to additional tests later conducted by Church officials.

When the early and later tests don't seem to have congruent results, and the official judgment of the Church is rendered as not being able to establish a supernatural (from God) or preternatural (from the devil) cause, but instead only provide natural explanations, it may give the false impression that the Catholic Church doesn't care about scientific inquiry or, due to politics or other reasons, suppresses results that appear supportive of mystical claims. The fact remains that there have been few credible apparition cases in the modern era of scientific testing, where there have been enough visions occurring over the course of a substantial period of time that they have both grabbed the Church's attention as potentially miraculous and allowed for the coordination and timing of scientific studies.

Thus far, while independent tests have rendered some tantalizing results, there are no Church-sanctioned scientific examinations in the modern era performed on alleged visionaries as part of an official ecclesiastical inquiry to establish a supernatural event. The Catholic Church will continue to apply the latest tools and techniques to cases in the future that merit its attention and official investigation.

In the meantime, we will close this chapter with a recurring theme from this text. While apparitions can strengthen the faith of God's children and have been known to convey important messages from heaven and spark pious devotions, we cannot place the foundation of our faith in such miraculous stories. A life of Christian virtue in communion with Christ's Church, receiving her sacraments, and loving God and neighbor must be the pillars of our faith. We should be wary of getting caught up in mystical phenomenon to the extent it complicates our daily lives as Catholics. Too often, apparitions are cases of fraud or psychological sicknesses, or even in some cases, acts of trickery by the demonic. We must always allow Holy Mother Church to review these cases and be patient as we wait on her judgment.

7

Eucharistic Miracles

The Mystery of Transubstantiation

At every Catholic Mass, when the priest pronounces the words of Jesus Christ at the Last Supper, "This is my body, which will be given up for you" and "This is the cup of my blood, the blood of the new and everlasting covenant," the host and the wine transform not symbolically but *truly* into the body and blood of Christ.

Some non-believers, Christians, and even some Catholics might find this doctrine a little more comfortable if it were assumed that Jesus was speaking symbolically and not literally. Some are not comfortable with this strange teaching that seems to border on cannibalism. This is true in our own time and in the time in which Christ taught, as the Gospel of John shows us:

> So Jesus said to them, "Truly, truly, I say to you, unless you eat the flesh of the Son of man and drink his blood, you have no life in you; he who eats my flesh and drinks my blood has eternal life, and I will raise him up at the last day. . . . Many of his disciples, when

they heard it, said, "This is a hard saying; who can listen to it?" But Jesus, knowing in himself that his disciples murmured at it, said to them, "Do you take offense at this? Then what if you were to see the Son of man ascending where he was before? It is the spirit that gives life, the flesh is of no avail; the words that I have spoken to you are spirit and life. But there are some of you that do not believe." For Jesus knew from the first who those were that did not believe, and who it was that should betray him. And he said, "This is why I told you that no one can come to me unless it is granted him by the Father." After this many of his disciples drew back and no longer went about with him. (Jn 6:53–54, 60–66)

Those disciples who "drew back and no longer went about with him" have descendants who follow in their path today, finding the Catholic Church's teaching on the Eucharist too much of a "hard saying" to believe.

But the Church stresses the importance and centrality of the Eucharist for the faithful: "The Eucharist is the source and summit of all Christian life. In the Eucharist, the sanctifying action of God in our regard and our worship of him reach their high point. It contains the whole spiritual good of the Church, Christ himself, our Pasch. Communion with divine life and unity of the People of God are both expressed and effected by the Eucharist. Through the Eucharistic celebration we are united already with the liturgy of heaven and we have a foretaste of eternal life."[70]

The famed theologian Saint Thomas Aquinas explained that the change which occurs to the bread and wine at the moment of consecration only involves its *substance*, while the *accidents*—the appearance of the bread and wine—remain unchanged. Thomas called this transubstantiation. This spiritual reality is a great mystery of our faith.

But on some rare occasions, it is not just the substance, or essence, of the bread and wine that changes. Sometimes, a few select souls have been fortunate enough to witness a change also in the appearance.

Types of Eucharistic Miracles

While the mystery of transubstantiation is considered miraculous by the faithful in its own right, there have been more than one hundred Eucharistic miracles of various sorts on top of that incredible "baseline" miracle throughout Christian history. The vast majority (90 percent) of historical cases have predictably been witnessed in Europe, with Italy (thirty-three), Spain (twenty), and France (eleven) making up a large portion of the cases.[71] The largest concentration of Eucharistic miracles occurred in the thirteenth, fourteenth, and fifteenth centuries, but—as with other types of miracles we have studied thus far—a rise in cases occurred in the twentieth century and beyond, with more cases than not (70 percent) being reported outside Europe. There has only been one approved occurrence on our own continent of North America: in Tixtla, Mexico, in 2006.[72]

Eucharistic miracles can be categorized under several different types—namely, the experiences of saints and mystics, inexplicable preservations, protection from danger, strange manifestations, and visible human flesh and blood. As we will see, some of these lend themselves to "proof" more than others. For example, saints like Saint Thomas Aquinas have seen visions of the Eucharist, which is difficult to examine scientifically. The phenomenon of *inedia*, or "Eucharistic fasting," where someone lives on the Eucharist alone for an extended period of time, allows for at least some chances of observation. German mystic Servant of God Therese Neumann (1898–1962), best-known for her stigmata, was observed in July 1927 by a medical doctor and four Franciscan nurses who kept a watch on her for two weeks straight while she consumed nothing but one consecrated host a day and suffered no adverse health effects.[73] Other saints to experience *inedia* include Saint Catherine of Siena (1347–1380), Blessed Alexandrina Maria da Costa (1904–1955), and Blessed Anne Catherine Emmerich (d. 1824).

There are also numerous stories of a consecrated Host surviving a perilous situation such as an earthquake, flood, fire, or theft. In 1750, a ciborium (made of gold) in a church tabernacle and the many consecrated hosts inside it were stolen from the Basilica of Saint Francis in Siena, Italy, while the priests and the faithful were gathered for the vigil of the feast of the Assumption. After the town prayed for the safe return of the Hosts, the thieves secretly returned the ciborium out of guilt. The Hosts were discovered stuffed in the church's poor box. All 348 whole Hosts and 6 halves were recovered. If the story ended there, we would say it was merely an example of conversion (of the hearts of the thieves). The miraculous nature of the story, however, stems from the fact that these hosts still survive to this day, showing no sign of mold or decay after two and a half centuries.

Then there have been some cases which involve a surprising "mark" appearing on a Host. On April 28, 2001, during adoration at a novena to Saint Jude at Saint Mary's in the Malankara Catholic Church in Chirattakonam, India, the parish priest and members of the congregation noticed several dark spots forming on the consecrated Host. After reserving it in the tabernacle for the week, the priest and congregation could make out the face of a bearded man with a crown of thorns. The image clarified over time, so much so that the local bishop accepted it as miraculous. Skeptics would assert that this is a case of red bread mold and pareidolia (seeing something meaningful in a random pattern). There is no way to deny this is possible, but it is very difficult to see the marks on the Host and not see the face of the suffering Christ. For the marks to take that pattern randomly is difficult to believe.

All of these strange instances point to a high probability of something happening beyond our normal laws of nature, but as we noted, there is little that can be done to verify them scientifically. Thankfully, that is not the case for the next kind we will examine.

The Miracle of Lanciano

Of all the Eucharistic miracles, the ones where flesh and blood are made visible on the Host are most conducive to scientific investigation. Of that sort, an instance in Lanciano, in the Abruzzo region of east central Italy, occurring around the year 750, is perhaps the most widely known and the most thoroughly investigated.

In the story known locally as Il Miracolo, one of the Basilian monks entered the church of Saint Longinus to celebrate Mass. His faith was weak and he had begun to have serious doubts about the Real Presence.

That day, though, when he pronounced the words of consecration, the white host suddenly warmed in his hands and turned pink, dark red, and fleshy. The wine in the chalice also darkened to a deep blood red. The priest was lost in wonder, and showing the miraculous manifestation to those gathered, his faith was restored.

While science will never be able to prove the efficacy of the sacraments and the power of the words of consecration themselves, it could examine this case to determine what exactly we were looking at.

The first objective quantitative study of this miraculous species (that we know of) was conducted in 1574 by Archbishop Antonio Gaspar Rodríguez. Even though sixteenth-century research had very limited capabilities, the bishop conducted a study that determined the five "globules" of blood in the chalice, despite being different sizes, all weighed the same amount. Still more, each individual globule, regardless of size, weighed the same amount as all five of them weighed together, or any other combination. Each weigh exactly 15.85 grams, and all parts together also weigh the same 15.85 grams. This "miracle of the weights" is considered to be a small miracle within a miracle.

In the eighteenth and nineteenth centuries, other examinations of the miracle were made, but twentieth-century science has rendered the clearest conclusions.

In 1971, the bishop of Chieti charged two doctors—Dr. Odoardo Linoli, a professor of anatomy, pathological histology, chemistry, and clinical microscopy, and former head of the Laboratory of Pathological Anatomy at the Hospital of Arezzo, and Dr. Ruggero Bertelli, retired professor of human anatomy at the University of Siena—with carrying out a thorough analysis of samples of the miracle. After running a battery of tests, they presented a detailed account of their results in *Quaderni Sclavo di Diagnostica Clinica e di Laboratori* in 1971:

1. The "miracle flesh" is truly meat consisting of the striated muscle tissue of the myocardium (muscular tissue of the heart) in the upper left ventricle.
2. The complete analysis of the individual molecules of the "miraculous blood" showed with objective, absolute certainty that it is real blood.
3. The immunological study showed with complete certainty that the flesh and blood are of human nature and that both belong to the same blood group, AB. This means the blood and flesh could be from the same person.
4. The proteins of the blood are broken down normally, according to the pattern of fresh blood.
5. There was no trace of salts or other preservative substances used in antiquity for mummification.

A few years later, a second, even more independent investigation further confirmed findings in research done by the World Health Organization. In 1973, the public health arm of the United Nations conducted a barrage of five hundred tests over a period of fifteen months. These tests confirmed that the miracle was the flesh of a human heart and human blood of the AB+ type. Both the flesh and blood were fresh living tissue. During testing, the samples from the miracle had responded to all the tests with the same reactions distinctive of living beings. This round of tests also confirmed the miracle of the weights.

The Miracle of Santarem

In the thirteenth century, in Santarem, Portugal, less than sixty kilometers due south of the famed Marian apparition site of Fatima, another dramatic miracle of this sort occurred.

Suspecting that her husband was unfaithful but unable to attain proof, a woman went to enlist the help of a sorceress. As payment for her services, the sorceress required a consecrated Host. The reasons for this are unknown, but it was presumably to perform some kind of sacrilege.

The woman agreed, and the next time she attended Mass, she placed a Host in her handkerchief. But on her way to meet the sorceress, the Host began to bleed; it bled so much, in fact, that she rushed home and hid it in a drawer. When a miraculous light was said to illuminate the drawer at night, she and her husband spent the night in prayer and, in the morning, called on the parish priest.

After he heard the woman's story, he retrieved the Host and led a procession with it back to Saint Stephen's. Canonical investigations were undertaken in 1340 and 1612, and on both occasions, the miracle was found to be authentic. Over the centuries, the host has appeared like fresh bloody tissue or as dry and hardened. The solidified blood is kept today in a glass vial in a reliquary at the shrine in Santarem above the main altar.

Testing for Authenticity

With these types of miracles, a similar protocol is always followed, at least in modern times. The inquiry is first begun by the local bishop if he deems it worthy of investigation. A sample of the tissue or species is then sent to an independent lab *with no disclosure of the source*. These tests determine if the sample is of human origin and reveal the blood group and type and muscle tissue type.

Such tests have, on occasion, provided enough insight to determine no miracle took place. For example, there have been cases of apparent Eucharistic miracles when a red discoloration is found on the consecrated Host, but through scientific examination, it has been determined to have another cause.

In 2015, a reddish substance began to appear on a host at Saint Francis Xavier Church in Kearns, Utah, a Salt Lake City suburb. During Holy Communion on November 8, a member of the congregation returned a consecrated Host to the celebrant that was incorrectly given to a young child who had not yet received her first Holy Communion. Not being able to distribute this particular Host to anyone else (for fear of spreading germs), the priest placed the Host in water to dissolve. After several days, it developed a red color which gave the appearance of bleeding. The diocesan administrator appointed an ad hoc committee, including experts in Catholic theology, canon law, molecular biology, and ministry, to examine it.[74] They determined that the red color was caused by mold, and a statement was released: "In November of 2015, it was alleged that a consecrated host . . . from Saint Francis Xavier Church in Kearns, Utah, appeared to be bleeding. A thorough investigation has concluded that the host did not bleed, but the change of appearance in the host was due to red bread mold [*Neurospora cressa*]. The consecrated host has been disposed of in a reverent manner, as is required."[75]

A fungus like *Neurospora cressa* is not unheard of on hosts since it is commonly found on bread, the substance before it becomes the Body of Our Lord. Similar to this is *Serratia marcescens*, a bacterium that can colonize bread and, due to its red pigmentation from the dye prodigiosin, produce stains sometimes resembling blood.

Although some cases have been nothing more than a discoloration due to mold or another source, some spectacular modern cases around the world have joined the likes of Lanciano, having been tested and shown to be true flesh and blood.

On December 8, 1991, at Mass at the Finca Marian Shrine in Betania, Venezuela, near the location of the Church-approved Marian apparition site related to Maria Esperanza de Bianchini, a priest broke the consecrated Host into four parts, consuming one part himself. One of those pieces began to show a red spot, from which a red substance eventually began exuding. The bishop of Los Teques requested a series of studies, which lead to five hundred tests by the World Health Organization. These tests confirmed that the blood of the priest did not match the blood found on the Eucharist, since some had wondered if he bled onto the Host. The blood type was found again to be AB and determined to be taken from a living heart. It is possible today to go see the miraculous Host in the Augustinian Recollects convent of the nuns of the Sacred Heart of Jesus in Los Teques.

On August 15, 1996, in Buenos Aires, Argentina, a local priest of the parish of Santa María, Padre Alejandro Pezet, claimed that after Mass, a communion Host was found discarded in the church. According to standard practice, the recovered Host was placed into a bowl of water to dissolve and then placed in the tabernacle. A reddish substance began to form more than a week later. It was then moved into a new tabernacle, where it continued to dissolve for eleven more days.[76] Permission was given by the local ordinary, Archbishop Jorge Bergoglio (the future Pope Francis), in October 1999 to take a sample for testing. Professor Ricardo Castañon Gomez, Dr. John Walker (professor at the University of Sydney), forensic pathologist Dr. Robert Lawrence, and Italian Professor Edoardo Linoli (who examined the Lanciano miracle), all participated in the initial studies of the sample.

On March 2, 2004, Professor Frederick Zugibe of Columbia University, an expert in forensic medicine of the heart, received the sample without disclosure of the source. Professor Zugibe identified the presence of intact white blood cells, which was indicative of dynamic activity (i.e., living tissue) when it was brought into the laboratory. He confirmed that the sample was of the AB+ blood type and was from the myocardium, specifically the upper left ventricle (as was also the case in Lanciano). The sample contained thrombi, which indicated to him that at certain moments the patient could not breathe for lack of oxygen and had been struck in the chest.[77] Nuclear DNA testing was conducted in three independent DNA labs but failed to produce a human genetic profile (which is normally easily obtained).[78] In 2006, the results were presented to Cardinal Jorge Maria Bergoglio, the future Pope Francis. The miraculous host is now on display in a monstrance and small shrine in the parish of Santa María for the faithful see and venerate.

In October 2006, in Tixtla, Mexico, during a retreat Mass at the Parish of Saint Martin of Tours, a consecrated Host was found to be effusing a reddish substance. An extensive scientific study was undertaken at the diocese to discern its cause and origin and to ensure there was no hoax being played. The examination showed it was not possible for the blood to have been placed on the host from an outside source, meaning it originated from *within*. As with other situations like this, the blood type was AB. It was reported that

> the reddish substance analyzed corresponds to blood in which there are hemoglobin and DNA of human origin. . . . Two studies conducted by eminent forensic experts with different methodologies have shown that the substance originates from the interior, excluding the hypothesis that someone could have placed it from the exterior. The blood type is AB, similar to the one found in the Host of Lanciano and in the Holy Shroud of Turin. A microscopic analysis of magnification and penetration reveals that the superior part of the blood has been coagulated since October 2006. Moreover, the underlying internal layers reveal, in February 2010, the presence of fresh blood. The event does not have a natural explanation.[79]

On Sunday, October 12, 2008, at 8:30 a.m., at Saint Anthony's Parish in Sokolka, Poland, a consecrated Host fell to the ground during the distribution of Communion. As is the standard practice, it was placed in a vasculum to dissolve and later be disposed of properly. This was done by the parish sacristan, Sister Julia Dubowska of the Congregation of the Eucharistic Sisters. At the end of the Mass, at the request of the pastor, Fr. Stanislaw Gniedziejko, she placed the container in the parish sacristy safe, a safe only she and the pastor had keys to.

A week later, she checked on the condition of the Host and noticed a discoloration. The pastor wondered if it was simply dirt, or a blood clot, and brought it to the attention of the metropolitan archbishop of Bialystok, Edward Ozorowski. The stained host was put back in the tabernacle after having been taken out of the water and placed on a small corporal. The host dried out naturally, maintaining the appearance of a blood stain or clot, and was kept there in secret for three years.

The archbishop eventually requested that a histopathological study be done on the Host and created an ecclesial commission. In the resulting inquiry, Professor Maria Elżbieta Sobaniec-Łotowska and Professor Stanisław Sulkowski, two specialists of pathological anatomy at the Medical University of Białystok, in independent tests and with the source unknown, found that a human cardiac muscle tissue from the upper left ventricle (as in the cases of Lanciano and Buenos Aires) had been joined to the Eucharist in an inseparable manner. The results of both independent studies were in perfect agreement that the structure of the transformed fragment of the host is identical to the myocardial (heart) tissue of a living person at death. The structure of the heart muscle fibers was inseparably connected with that of the "bread" in a manner that defied human abilities according to the declaration of Professor Maria Sobaniec-Lotowska.[80] This integration of substances was validated by an electron microscope down to the size of the diameter of a water molecule.[81]

In his official statement, the Metropolitan Curia of Bialystok declared: "The Sokolka event is not opposed to the faith of the Church; rather, it confirms it. The Church professes that, after the words of consecration, by the power of the Holy Spirit, the bread is transformed into the Body of Christ, and the wine into His Blood. Additionally, this is an invitation for all ministers of the Eucharist to distribute the Body of the Lord with faith and care, and for the faithful to receive Him with adoration."[82]

Finally, on Christmas Day 2013, at Saint Jack Parish in Legnica, Poland, after Msgr. Zbigniew Kiernikowski retrieved a fumbled consecrated Host from the floor and placed it in water to dissolve, a reddish color began to show. A commission assembled by the former bishop of Legnica, Stefan Cichy, in February 2014 began testing it in Szichen, Poland. In 2016, the results were announced with the determination that the sample contained striated heart tissue of human origin. The Department of Forensic Medicine stated that "the histopathological tissue fragments were found containing fragmented part of the skeletal muscle. . . . The whole image . . . is the most similar to the heart muscle . . . with the changes that often are accompanied by the agony" of death.[83]

Bishop Zbigniew Kiernikowski of the Diocese of Legnica gave his approval of the phenomena with the establishment of a small shrine within the church for the faithful to visit.

It is interesting to note that in all these cases, a similar pattern has been discovered: human blood in the group AB (also the blood type found on the purported burial cloth of Christ, the Shroud of Turin), transmutation of the substance of the Host to the substance of heart tissue, and signs of distress in the patient. The consistency of these findings, and the connection to the distress Christ would have faced during his passion, add to the already astounding and inexplicable phenomenon of the appearance of blood and fleshy tissue, *and only after the Host has been consecrated.* No DNA profile has been able to be obtained from any of the samples, perhaps due to contamination.

As with the other types of miracles we have examined, there are many cases where science can explain what happened with a natural explanation. But on some very rare occasions, there have been authentic cases that science cannot explain.

Another question is fair to ask: Could these seemingly miraculous cases have been the result of a hoax? It seems extremely unlikely. White blood cells do not survive the death of a body, so to get a sample of heart tissue with white blood cells embedded in the ventricle wall due to severe trauma (as has been found in cases of Eucharistic miracles), the sample would need to be taken from the heart of a living person *while the heart is still beating.* Moreover, achieving the transmutation of the two interwoven substances—bread and heart tissue—on a microscopic level seems to go beyond human capabilities. How far would the Catholic Church need to go to perpetrate such a fraud?

Whatever the case, the final conclusion by a local bishop in the study of a possible Eucharistic miracle must follow an unbiased study by a panel of experts, as demonstrated with these examples. While these examinations may establish the presence of flesh and blood, there is, of course, no scientific test for the presence of the soul and divinity of Jesus Christ, which are transcendent properties that extend beyond the organic, physical world. If the bishop makes a declaration of approval, it is intended to demonstrate to the faithful that God continues to work miracles in our age and reaffirms this most challenging of Catholic beliefs: that the bread and wine have been transformed into the body, blood, soul, and divinity of Jesus Christ.

Such miracles inspire Catholics and their belief in the Real Presence and the recitation of affirmations of faith, such as the traditional prayer "O Sacrament Most Holy, O Sacrament Divine, may all praise and thanksgiving, be every moment Thine."

8

Weeping Statues and Icons

Miracles Surrounding Statues and Icons

Toward the end of the sixth century, Rome was struck by a plague that claimed thousands of lives, including the life of Pope Pelagius II. His successor, Pope Saint Gregory the Great (c. 540–604) prayed that the Roman people be delivered from this scourge and called for a procession to take place at dawn. The procession of the faithful singing and praying surrounded the ancient mausoleum of the Roman emperor Hadrian, a large fortress on the Tiber River, and followed Saint Gregory, who carried an icon of the Virgin Mary attributed to Saint Luke. According to pious legend, Saint Michael the Archangel appeared miraculously on the battlements of Hadrian's mausoleum, standing upon the cupola with his flaming sword. The spread of the plague ceased almost immediately, and the people paid homage and expressed their gratitude to Saint Michael and the Blessed Virgin, attributing the miracle to the icon.

This is just one example of the miracles that have been said to surround Catholic statues and icons. Most commonly, the miracles related to icons have been those events where tears have been claimed to emanate from a statue or image of the Virgin Mary, and so that will be the focus of this chapter. Let us run briefly and quickly through a list of miracles recorded throughout the history of the Church:

- In 1170, a coalition of forces of land owning princes, headed by a son of Prince Andrew Bogoliubsky of Suzdal, marched to the walls of the city of Novgorod. When the people of Novgorod prayed for help from heaven, Elias the bishop heard a wondrous voice commanding that the icon of the Most Holy Theotokos be taken out of the church and carried about on the city walls. When they processed the icon, the attackers fired a volley of arrows at the procession, and one of them pierced the face of the Mother of God. Tears trickled from her eyes, and the icon turned its face towards the city. After this divine sign, an inexpressible terror suddenly fell upon the invaders. They began to strike one another, and the people of Novgorod fearlessly fought and won the victory.

- In 1486, several pious women of Cravegna, Italy, collected alms to create a *virgo lactans* image painted on the right side of the façade of the church. It would depict the Madonna seated on a throne with the infant Child in the center. On December 20, 1493, the sacristan of the church of San Giulio, Lorenzo di Francesco di Giovan, noticed that during the hour of vespers, the image of the Madonna started to emit tears from both eyes and the face became flooded. The same thing occurred on the right eye of the Child. The entire face and other exposed parts of the figure of the Madonna and Child appeared then as blankets of fresh sweat. The event lasted the next two days. Even though everything else was frozen in the cold weather, the tears flowing out of the sacred image did not freeze.

- According to tradition, on June 2, 1511, a shepherdess in Ponte Nossa, Italy was staring at a Marian icon and saw the face change, opening and closing her eyes to weep blood. She heard a voice that told her to call the other people in order to observe the miracle as well as to build a new church. The witnesses' testimony was then collected by a notary and put in writing. The new church was completed on the site in 1533.

- When the region around Mutxamel (a municipality in Spain) encountered a severe drought in 1545, the townspeople carried their Virgin image in procession three miles south to Santa Faz, to the Saint Veronica monastery shrine. On the return trip, Fr. Lloréns Boix suddenly found the image too heavy to carry. Near San Juan, he lifted the protective veil to examine the image and discovered that the Virgin's left eye was shedding a tear. The rains came soon afterwards. The fiesta of La Llágrima, the Tear, is celebrated annually on March 1 in commemoration of this miracle.

- In 1546, in a street fight near the shrine of the Madonna del Portico d'Ottavia, near a Roman ghetto, one man begged another to spare his life for love of the Virgin Mary, who was seen in a nearby fres-

co. When his opponent showed him mercy, he literally stabbed him in the back. The nearby image
wept for three days following this act of treachery.
The fifteenth-century fresco was then moved into
the nearby church of San Salvatore de Cacabariis.
In 1612, church reconstruction began, and in 1616,
the image was reinstalled and the church rededicated
to the Weeping Madonna. The image of Mother and
Child was crowned on May 20, 1643.

- To celebrate his release in 1696 from his captivity as
a prisoner of war by the Turks, Laszlo Csigri commis-
sioned a wooden icon of the Virgin and Child in his
hometown of Pócs, Hungary. On November 4, the
icon began to shed tears, and when a priest held up a
dying child to those tears, he was miraculously healed.

- From January 6 to February 16, 1717, in Sajópál-
fala, a town in northeastern Hungary that was destroyed and deserted during the Turkish occupation
of the fifteenth century, a painting of the Madonna
and Child perspired and wept bloody tears in the
town's church. The picture was then taken to Eger by
the investigating bishop. It stayed in the Franciscan
church, becoming the central element of an annual
pilgrimage to Our Lady of Sorrows on her feast.

- The parish church of Steinbach (Germany), in 1728,
acquired a set of painted wooded statues of the Crucifixion, the Sorrowful Mother, and Saint John. Two
years later, parishioners gave accounts that the statue
of Our Lady of Sorrows was moving its eyes, crying,
and changing complexion. Miracles and healings

also accompanied the prodigy. The bishop of the diocese established a formal investigation that found the miracles valid in 1734.

- On the evening of December 16, 1857, a terrible earthquake struck the population of Basilicata, Italy, and the neighboring regions. The next day, the residents of Paterno decided to bring the statue of the Madonna del Carmine into the streets. Legend has it that as soon as the procession reached the present district Marsh, in front of the destroyed houses and carts full of corpses, Mary turned her face, and her eyes shed tears of blood. The miraculous event is commemorated every year on December 17.

- On March 2, 1877, seven monks remained in the monastery church at Mount Athos in Greece after prayers. They were astonished to see tears flowing from the right eye of the icon and collecting on the frame. Then a single large tear came from the left eye. The monks wiped the tears from the icon's face and then left the church and locked the doors behind them. Three hours later, they returned for Vespers and saw traces of tears on the icon and a single tear in the left eye.

Modern Cases

One may have noticed that all these instances happened centuries ago. But even in modern times, miraculous statues continue to manifest the phenomenon of tears.

One of the most fascinating cases in history occurred in 1973 when a deaf nun named Sr. Agnes Sasagawa, living in

the remote area of Yuzawadai, outside Akita, Japan, encountered a bright light emanating from the tabernacle in her
convent's chapel on several occasions. She reported that she
saw her guardian angel, and subsequently, an illuminated
three-foot-high wooden statue of Our Lady of All Nations
bled from its hand. During the course of eight years and over
one hundred messages, the statue began to weep as well, a
phenomenon witnessed by as many as two thousand people
and broadcast on Japanese national television. Scientific tests
would show that they were human tears and blood. Tears
and liquid from the statue were gathered and sent for study
to the laboratories of Akita University in the Department
of Biochemistry. Additionally, samples were examined in a
blind study by a non-Christian named Dr. Kaoru Sagisaka, a
forensic specialist in legal medicine in the faculty of medicine
at the University of Akita. The liquid was shown to be identical to human tears, type AB. The blood was confirmed to be
of human origin—type B—and the sweat human type AB.

The investigation by the Catholic Church originally rendered a *non constat* judgment, which came from a commission of inquiry initiated by Bishop John Shojiro of Niigata.
When Bishop Ito consulted with Cardinal Ratzinger (later
Pope Benedict XVI), the head of the Congregation for the
Doctrine of the Faith, Ito expressed such a strong belief in
the authenticity of the events that he was encouraged by
Ratzinger to form a second commission, after which Ito
declared on April 22, 1984: "After the inquiries conducted
up to the present day, one cannot deny the supernatural
character of a series of unexplainable events relative to the
statue of the Virgin honored at Akita (Diocese of Niigata).

Consequently, I authorize that all of the diocese entrusted to me venerate the Holy Mother of Akita."

He also commented on the permanent restoration of Sister Agnes's hearing, a promise made by the angel:

> Effectively on the last Sunday of the month of Mary, the 30th of May, 1982, Feast of Pentecost, at the moment of Benediction of the Blessed Sacrament her ears were cured completely and instantly. That same evening she telephoned me and we conversed normally. On the following 14 of June, I visited Doctor Arai of the Eye and Ear Division of the Hospital of the Red Cross of Akita who had verified the complete deafness of Sr. Agnes Sasagawa at the moment she arrived in Akita nine years before. I asked his impression. He expressed his amazement at this complete cure. Doctor Sawada of the Rosai Hospital of Joetsu who had been the first to examine her when she became deaf, has now issued a medical certificate dated June 3rd, 1982, attesting that following minute examinations of her auditive capacities, he certifies that there is no further anomaly in the two ears of Sr. Agnes Sasagawa.[84]

The Akita statue phenomenon remains controversial due to the dramatic and negative messages about apocalyptic natural disasters and the future of the Church ("cardinals opposing cardinals, bishops against bishops").[85] It remains debated whether Bishop Ito had given approval most specifically to the bleeding statue related events of Akita verified by science or to the entirety of the events, including the content of the messages.

The president of the Japanese Bishops' Conference, Peter Seiichi Shirayanagi, in a 1990 interview with the Catholic magazine *30 Days*, said, "The events of Akita are no longer to be taken seriously. We think they do not now have a great significance for the Church and Japanese society."[86] Nonetheless, Our Lady of Akita is still considered an approved phenomenon by the Church, and many continue to venerate her.

The visionary of Akita, Sr. Agnes Sasagawa, chose to withdraw from the public eye and live in private in her later years.

Another modern case worth highlighting has been called the greatest occurrence of weeping statues in the history of the Church.[87]

In 1992, thousands of visitors—including local, national, and international media—began to flock to Saint Elizabeth Ann Seton Church in Lake Ridge, Virginia, where eyewitness accounts claimed that the associate pastor there, Fr. James Bruse, was a stigmatic bearing the wounds of Christ on his wrists and feet. Still more, it was said that he caused statues of the Virgin Mary to weep tears of blood. On many occasions, a statue of the Virgin Mary in the church began to cry, as did several other statues on the parish grounds, during, before, or after one of his Masses. Father Bruse sometimes only had to be in a statue's vicinity for the crying to begin, even one in a completely different church.

Despite the statues weeping into the hands of witnesses, and even in the presence of John R. Keating, bishop of Arlington, the miracles were never examined by the chancery. All movements towards an investigation were shut down due to there being no divine messages to consider and in the hopes of quelling the circus-like atmosphere.[88]

While some cases like this do not receive as much attention from Church authorities as we may like (or at least enough to satisfy our own curiosity), other instances receive the full attention of a scientific investigation.

In the summer of 2018, news of a miracle spread on various Catholic websites about a bronze statue of Our Lady of Guadalupe weeping tears at the Our Lady of Guadalupe parish in Hobbes, New Mexico. Huge crowds began to come from hundreds of miles away to witness the phenomena and capture it on their smart phones (and subsequently post on Facebook or other social media outlets). The interest was so great that secular media—even the *Washington Post*—published stories on the events.

All told, the statue was said to have wept on four separate occasions, enough that the local diocese of Las Cruces initiated an investigation. The local bishop, Oscar Cantú, released an official statement in 2019 declaring the tears naturally inexplicable, saying, "We have not discerned natural causes for the statue's emitting of liquid."[89]

During the investigation, the diocese hired investigators to monitor the church with twenty-four-hour surveillance, take x-rays of the statue to try to identify any internal ductwork issues, and check the premises for leaky pipes overhead. They also contacted the company in Mexico that created the statue and interviewed Ricardo Flores-Kastanis, owner of Our Lady of Guadalupe Art, who assured them that the same traditional lost-wax casting process was used on this particular statue (now affectionately known amongst his employees as *La Milagrosa*, "The Miraculous") that was used on hundreds of others they produced. When the chemical analysis came back, it was revealed that the tears were made of rose-scented olive oil, which was different from the oil used in the baptismal chrism found in the church.

Interestingly enough, oil is one of the common substances found in weeping icons. Oil, of course, is a sign of healing and strength, and is symbolic of the Holy Spirit. Holy chrism—used in anointing, which is the sacramental sign and seal of the Holy Spirit—is found in the rites of Baptism, Confirmation, Anointing of the Sick, and Holy Orders.

Outside the Roman Church, we see that most Orthodox icons purported to exude a liquid also give off an oil-based substance. One famous modern case involved a woman named Myrna Nazzour, a native of Damascus. On November 27, 1982, oil started to exude from a small replica of the icon of the Virgin of Kazan bought by her husband, Nicolas, in July of 1980. This oozing of the icon reportedly followed the rhythm of the liturgical cycle, occurring only on major feast days, and lasted until November 26, 1990. Over the course of a decade, the oil was collected and distributed amongst the many people who came to venerate the icon. The substance was tested by scientists and found to be 100 percent pure olive oil.[90] The resulting report of the chromatography examination which was designed to determine the different components of the oil drew attention to the impossibility of the phenomena:

> We analyzed the different components, sterol and acid fats. For the acid fats, when we add all the elements, we obtain 100% which is compatible with the composition of olive oil. For sterol, the results are similar

except for this sample analyzed in Paris. There exists, in addition to the sterol of vegetal origin, a trace of cholesterol, whose origin can be of human or animal nature. This fact could be explained if the analyzed oil was collected from human skin: traces of perspiration can justify this trace of cholesterol, because sweat contains it. Nevertheless, coming from a piece of paper, it is just as unexplainable that vegetal oil or cholesterol become the seat of emission 'ex-nihilo', that is to say, without the contribution of natural substances.[91]

When the icon was transferred to the Byzantine Greek-Orthodox church of the Holy Cross, which was five hundred yards from the Nazzour house, on January 9, 1983, it reportedly ceased to exude oil.[92] Myrna later experienced additional supernatural phenomena, claiming visions of Mary and experiencing the manifestation of the wounds of Christ on her hands, feet, and forehead, oftentimes in the presence of scientists monitoring her. Since this case took place outside the Catholic Church, no study or ruling from Rome has ever taken place.

A Case of Approval: The Weeping Madonna of Syracuse

Weeping statues are not often definitively approved as miraculous in modern times; more typically, even the more convincing cases are simply described as being without natural explanation. A notable exception is that of the Weeping Madonna from Syracuse, Italy, in 1953, which enjoys the full recognition of the Catholic Church. This particular image is a mass-produced plaster plaque of the Immaculate Heart of Mary made in Tuscany by Amilcare Santini. It was given to Antonina and Angelo Iannuso on the occasion of their wedding on March 21, 1953. When they returned home, they hung the image on their bedroom wall.

Antonina soon became pregnant and was afflicted with severe toxemia that caused convulsions and vision problems. (She recovered completely and gave birth to a healthy son on December 25, 1953.) On Saturday, August 29, 1953, at 3:00 a.m., Antonina was stricken with a seizure resulting in her blindness. When her sight returned five hours later, she looked upon the Madonna, which was actively weeping tears that dripped off the image and onto the bed. The neighbors came in and confirmed the tears, which continued for four days.

The image was removed from the wall to help rule out a leaky pipe, and tests showed that there was no internal reservoir. Even after the tears were wiped away, new ones immediately reappeared. Crowds gathered in the streets around the house waiting for a chance to get inside to see the phenomena. They hung the plaque outside their house to avoid the crowds coming inside, and when the crowds still were too much of an infringement, it was taken to the police station. After forty minutes there, the tears dried up, and it was returned to the Iannusos' house. Early the next morning, the weeping image was placed on a cushion and displayed for those waiting in the streets all night. The following day, the plaque was nailed above the main door. The crowds collected the tears on pieces of cloth and swabs of cotton, with many claiming miraculous healings.

An investigative commission from the chancery was assembled with four scientists and three witnesses, who all arrived at the Iannuso home on Tuesday, September 1, to examine the prodigy. They found no pores or irregularities on the smoothly painted and varnished surface of the artwork, and on the reverse side, the unfinished gypsum was found to be dry. They collected a sample of actively falling tears for analysis using a sterilized pipette, placing the liquid in an uncontaminated vial that was taken to the laboratory to be examined by doctors and chemists. After this investigation, the plaque continued weeping for another fifty-one minutes, but at 11:40 a.m., the tears finally stopped completely.

The sample of the tears was scientifically compared to tears from an adult and a child. The examining doctors reached this conclusion in their report signed and dated September 9, 1953: "The liquid examined is shown to be made up of a watery solution of sodium chloride in which traces of protein and nuclei of a silver composition of excretory substances of the quaternary type, the same as found in the human secretions used as a comparison during the analysis. The appearance, the alkalinity and the composition induce one to consider the liquid examined analogous to human tears."[93]

The tears had been seen, the soaked cloths touched, and the saltiness taste-tested by Catholic and non-Catholic witnesses in multiple locations, ruling out the possibility of mass delusion. Condensation was also eliminated as a possible cause, as neither the entire image nor any nearby objects were wet (only the corners of the eyes). To further stress the authenticity, the statue actively weeping was caught on film, the first time in history that such an event was recorded on camera.

The archbishop of Syracuse visited the Iannuso home to examine the image and returned another day to recite the Rosary with the crowd, while the archbishop of Palermo, Ernesto Cardinal Ruffini, affirmed, "After careful sifting the numerous reports, after having noted the positive results of the diligent chemical analysis under which the tears gathered were examined, we have unanimously announced the judgment that the reality of the facts cannot be put in doubt."[94]

The medical commission established on October 7, 1953, to scientifically examine the healings related to the statue decided that 105 of 290 claims were deemed to be of "special interest," or likely miracles.

The bishops of Sicily, after examining the report finding the tears to be of human origin, declared on December 11, 1953, that the weeping was miraculous. A week later, *L'Osservatore Romano* (the official newspaper of the Vatican) reported their "sincere desire that this manifestation of our heavenly Mother may inspire the whole world with a true spirit of penance, and more fervent devotion to the Immaculate Heart of Mary. It is likewise their wish that a spiritual edifice be erected to commemorate the miracle."[95]

Pope Pius XII, in a radio broadcast on October 17, 1954, said, "We acknowledge the unanimous declaration of the Episcopal Conference held in Sicily on the reality of the event. Will men understand the mysterious language of those tears?"[96]

On November 6, 1994, the great basilica of Santuario Madonna Delle Lacrima (Shrine of Our Lady of the Tears) was dedicated by Pope John Paul II, who stated, "The tears of the Madonna belong to the order of signs. She is a mother crying when she sees her children threatened by a spiritual or physical evil."[97]

The miracle of the tears is celebrated in Sicily even today. The Iannuso home is now an oratory and site of many Masses. The basilica was built especially to accommodate the people—including three popes—who have continued to come to venerate the miraculous icon.

Taken as a whole, the long history and tradition of weeping statues continuing on into our modern day reaffirms the reality of these occurrences. While many have occurred in an era before scientific testing became the norm, and certainly some cases can now be attributed to natural causes, the great preponderance of these events establishes that this is an actual phenomenon that science cannot always explain.

Without audible messages imparted from heaven in most cases, beyond not knowing *how* it happens, perhaps the larger question is *why* it happens. Maybe it is different in every case, but perhaps God allows these manifestations to grab the attention of the faithful and provide an opportunity for internal reflection and evaluation on how each person might better authentically live out the virtues of the Christian life.

9

The Stigmata

Blessing or Curse?

Generally, when we think of a miracle, we associate the event with something good happening, like the healing of a physical ailment. It is fair to wonder if the stigmata—the phenomenon certain individuals (stigmatics) have where they mystically exhibit the wounds of Christ in their hands, and sometimes on their feet, forehead, or side—is a true miracle. If it were to happen to us, would we see it as a blessing or a curse, considering it brings with it great suffering?

Catholic theology tells us that suffering, in all cases and most especially in the case of the stigmata, is, in a way, a blessing because it is God's way of purifying us of self-love. It is a means to holiness and of reaching heaven if we accept it with faith and trust.

The Catholic Dictionary tells us that "the Church considers the three hundred recorded manifestations of the stigmata as signs of particular favor by the Lord," who allows certain individuals to participate physically in the suffering of the Crucifixion. These mystics have also united themselves with the profound suffering of Christ on a deep spiritual level as well. Their participation in his passion—physically and spiritually—is considered a distinct and rare *privilege* granted by the Lord to a small number of saints in history. (God certainly has a funny way of showing his favor!)

Since the stigmata can often bring fame and attention, just as with other miraculous claims, there is always the danger of deception. But as we will see, the Catholic Church's examination of alleged cases of the stigmata relies heavily on thorough medical examinations to rule out scams and frauds.

The authentic cases, though, provide a witness and serve as a reminder of what Christ endured, and give us a sign from heaven that can strengthen our faith. Let us examine this mystical phenomenon now.

The History and Science of the Stigmata

Tradition seems to indicate that the very first true stigmatic in recorded history was Saint Francis of Assisi (1182–1226). Art throughout the ages, including Giotto's *Saint Francis Receiving the Stigmata*, has depicted the great patron saint of Italy and founder of the Franciscans in this ecstatic moment of being marked with the wounds of Christ.[98] A man known as Brother Leo, who had been with Francis at the time, provided the first clear account of the stigmata phenomenon occurring on September 14, 1224, the feast of the Exaltation of the Cross: "Suddenly he saw a vision of a seraph, a six-winged angel on a cross. This angel gave him the gift of the five wounds of Christ."

Some might point to the words of Saint Paul in Galatians 6:17: "I bear on my body the marks of Jesus." But without the benefit of tradition giving us the true meaning of these words, we cannot say for sure if Paul was a stigmatic.

Whether or not Francis was the first is up for debate, but he is certainly counted amongst the few hundred stigmatics in recorded history.[99] Arguably the most well-known today and the first priest to exhibit the wounds was Saint Pio. Most stigmatics follow a consistent profile, as they are not only Catholics but typically (as many as 66 percent)[100] have entered religious life. Historically, they have come from traditionally Catholic countries, with the vast majority of cases being reported from Italy (more than a third) and most of the others stemming from Spain, France, and Portugal.[101]

Throughout history, most stigmatics—as many as 80 percent[102]—have been women, though in the last hundred years the distribution is more balanced (only 55 percent women). No viable scientific explanation has been hypothesized for this, but it is interesting to note that this trend corresponds to the majority of visionaries being female as well. Many stigmatics themselves are associated with other mystical phenomena, such as experiencing visions or surviving on the Eucharist alone (inedia).

The presence of these wounds—or stigmata "marks"—is often (mistakenly) taken to be a guaranteed divine sign of holiness conferred on a living person. While the famed stigmata of Padre Pio is celebrated with an annual commemoration by the Catholic Church, as a general practice, these wounds are not taken into account during the canonization process. These marks—while most typically found on saintly persons—are not a *guarantee* of a practiced life of virtue. Instances of stigmata have the potential for causing great scandal and embarrassment. When the Church investigates a case of stigmata, she is motivated to exclude the possibility of a supernatural cause and never seeks to approve an ongoing case. The best result could be a wait-and-see stance whereby Church officials might monitor the situation over the course of years.

When the Church begins an investigation of a stigmata, care is taken to observe the humility of the person displaying the wounds and places the person under medical observation. The wounds must be determined to:

- not be self-inflicted,
- have no signs of infection or malignancy,
- have no other explanatory skin disease,
- have no other natural causes,
- have no sign of active wound healing,
- be chronic,
- be symmetrical wounds on the volar and dorsal hands,
- and be consistent with the wounds of Christ.

The dermatologist or specialist of wounds would inquire with the patient about the source of the wounds to make sure there is no manipulation by the patient and to take measurements of the diameter of each wound and location. The following presentations would need to be observed:

- No signs of lichenification (suggestive of recurrent injury)

- No signs of peripheral contracture (suggestive of a healing wound)
- No jagged or angulated edges (suggestive of a factitial etiology)
- Normal skin pigmentation and dermoglyphic lines in the center of the rings (where the initial lesions were reported to begin)
- No signs of scarring
- No signs of factitial disease

Since we have already mentioned Padre Pio and how he is now today the most well-known stigmatic, it would do us well to examine his case.

Saint Pio of Pietrelcina

Francesco Forgione was born on May 25, 1887 in the small town of Pietrelcina, located in southern Italy. He came from a devout Catholic family of farmers and was himself a child shepherd, tending flocks in the surrounding fields. It is said that he experienced mystical visions, and by the age of five, he was adamant that he wanted to devote his life to God.

He made good on his word by joining a Capuchin friary at the young age of fifteen, taking the name Pio. His journey to the priesthood was slowed by ill health, including loss of appetite, insomnia, exhaustion, fainting spells, and migraines, but he was ordained in 1910.

The life of this holy man is one of the most unique and fascinating in the history of the Church (including stories of bilocation), but since our present concern is his stigmata, we will focus our discussion on that.

The exact date for when his stigmata appeared is unclear. In his letters, we read that he began to experience pain early in his priesthood without understanding the source, and he soon began to discern red marks on his hands. Eventually, the wounds became more pronounced, and he went on to bear the stigmata for fifty years, until the end of his life. His fame spread all over, which he greatly resisted. In addition to the physical pain, he experienced accusations of being a fraud, even within the Church. Seeing it as the will of God, he agreed to have studies conducted on his wounds.

Saint Pio underwent his first investigation into the authenticity of his stigmata for eight days starting on June 14, 1921 by the Holy Office (now Congregation for the Doctrine of the Faith). Bishop Carlo Raffaello Rossi was named the investigator and visited Padre Pio to examine his life and the origin of his wounds.

In his report, Bishop Rossi observed Padre Pio in detail, noting the way he cared for his fellow Capuchins and spent long hours every day in the confessional. He also had an "extraordinary devotion" to the Mass.

Rossi's interview of Padre Pio consisted of 142 questions, which were answered under oath. The man being interrogated displayed consistency and integrity. But it was the presence of the unexplainable, such as the perfume-like scents emanating from his wounds, that lead to further suggestion of his case being authentic.

In his own words, speaking about his stigmata, Padre Pio revealed:

On September 20, 1918 after celebrating Mass, while
I was giving thanks in the Choir, I was repeatedly over-
come by trembling. Later I became calm again and I
saw our Lord as if He were on the cross—but I did
not see if He did have a cross—lamenting the lack of
response from mankind, especially from those consecrated to Him who are His favorites. He was showing
that He was suffering and that He desired to unite
souls to His Passion. He invited me to enter into His
sufferings and to mediate upon them: and at the same
time to concern myself with the health of the brothers.
Immediately I felt full of compassion for the sufferings
of the Lord and I asked Him what I could do. I heard
this voice: "I unite you to my Passion." And immediately, the vision having disappeared, I came to and I
saw these signs from which blood was flowing. I did
not have them before.[103]

Padre Pio typically wore fingerless gloves to hide his wounds
from the public eye and never desired fame and attention.
But he subjected himself to many investigations over the
years, including examinations of his wounds by Bishop Rossi.
Physicians found nothing out of the ordinary in his skeletal
structure and noted the smoothness of the wounds and the
lack of edema (swelling caused by excess fluid trapped in
the body's tissue) that would have been expected.[104] Bishop
Rossi concluded that the wounds were not "the work of the
devil," nor were they the result of "deceit, fraud or a mali-
cious or evil ability. Much less were they the result of external
suggestion, nor do I consider them to be the result of suggestion." He believed he had confirmation of Padre Pio bearing

a true case of the stigmata and put to rest accusations that his wounds were self-inflicted. (The accusation was that he used carbolic acid to mutilate himself, supposedly obtained from a local pharmacy for the sterilization of needles used to fight the Spanish flu.) It was during the thorough investigations of Padre Pio's beatification process that these accusations were found to be without merit.[105]

Saint Pio was canonized on June 16, 2002 by Pope St. John Paul II. But we must not forget that his sainthood is founded upon his heroic holiness and not the mystical phenomenon of his stigmata. The reader would do well to go read about the entirety of his life.

More Cases from Modern History

While Padre Pio is the most well-known modern case of a person bearing the wounds of Christ, there have been others cases identified around the world in recent times.

Starting in 1983, Myrna Nazzour of Damascus had stigmata wounds open and close on her head, hands, feet, left side, and abdomen on Holy Thursday (on the coincidence of the Eastern and Western Churches celebrating Easter on the same day). Some have taken this to be a sign of Jesus's wish in the Gospel of John for Christian unity: *"ut unum sint"* ("that they may be one"; Jn 17:11).

The spontaneous opening and closing of Myrna's wounds were recorded on film, and the event has been studied thoroughly by several scientists and doctors.[106] One 2005 study on Myrna performed at Ulleval University Hospital in Oslo, Norway, tried to determine the origins of her wounds. It had been theorized that diseases involving maldistribution of microcirculation (such as erythromelalgia) could be the cause of this phenomena. In order to perform such an analysis, the history of the patient was considered and she was under clinical observation for the entire duration of the stigmatization—that is, before the wounds manifested and after they healed.

The blood from her wounds was compared to her venous blood and both were genotyped. Circulatory measures were undertaken with a perfusion scanner, spectroscopy, and impedance (testing of the elastic properties of the arteries and the vessel dimensions), and photo documentation from a microscope and external camera was gathered. Her saturation measures remained normal, and there was a significant rise in impedance. Since the measurements of blood flow lacked the characteristics of an erythromelalgian reaction (a rare condition that causes episodes of burning pain and redness in the feet, and sometimes the hands, arms, legs, ears, and face) and were similar to findings from the control study, local hypoxia (lower-than-normal concentrations of oxygen in arterial blood) was ruled out, and it was concluded that Myrna did not experience these wounds due to erythromelalgia.

The non-medical folks among us may not be able to understand every aspect of these studies. Nonetheless, the findings seemed to show that her case was authentic. Dr. Antoine Mansour of the UCLA School of Medicine, after personally observing Myrna, wrote a report in 1990. In his notes, he described the blood of the wounds as appearing bright red, oxygenated, and likely arterial in nature. He also observed, but could not scientifically explain, their rapid healing: "I saw the opening of the wounds of the exposed feet and hands in front of me. No games here."[107]

Dr. Philippe Loron, a neurologist at the Salpêtrière in France, examined Myrna as well. He reports, "The opening of the wounds was spontaneous without foreign object, without any suspicious move from Myrna nor from anyone present in the room, as if the skin was opening from the interior and exploding."[108]

Nazzour is Greek-Orthodox and has promoted the message that "Christians should pray for peace, love one another and pray for the unity of the Christian churches."[109] As a result of her being outside its jurisdiction, the Roman Catholic Church has neither undertaken an investigation or rendered a judgment about the apparitions, the exuding of oil from the associated Our Lady of Soufanieh icon, or the phenomena of her stigmata. The Catholic Church is well familiar with these occurrences (Pope Francis had an audience with her in 2018), and in typical fashion, she will not make a positive ruling on a person claiming to exhibit the stigmata while that person is still alive. In cases of fraud, the Church will swiftly render a negative judgment and provide guidelines in order to protect the Catholic faithful from false claims.

Another modern case of stigmata involved Dina Basher, a Catholic from Iraq who claimed to experience apparitions of Christ, the Virgin Mary, angels, and various saints beginning on the feast of the Assumption in Mosul in 1991. Her ecstasies—which supposedly gave her a sharing in Christ's passion—were reported to last anywhere from ten minutes to three hours, or even longer. Similar to Myrna Nazzour, Dina's hands and sometimes her face were said to exude a mysterious fragrant oil beginning on September 29, 1991, and many healing miracles began to happen in her presence.

The stigmata—including a large round but jagged wound on her forehead—began to manifest in front of many witnesses in Mansur where, at the request of the local bishop, doctors studied her. The psychiatrists didn't believe the wounds to be a "psychosomatic" manifestation (physical wounds being caused by mental stress). After her brain scans and X-rays were normal and the doctors deemed the events to be "beyond nature's capability," her patriarch and the bishop of Baghdad declared the phenomena to be of supernatural origin.[110]

Skepticism Surrounding the Stigmata

Considering the dramatic nature of the stigmata phenomenon, it is not surprising that there would be plenty of skeptics and nonbelievers. Their doubt stems from several avenues.

Most people who question stigmata cases presume the person in question is harming himself (or herself). It is true that the most common type of false stigmata is the self-inflicted variety. Self-mutilation due to psychological disorders or misguided piety accounts for the near entirety of all alleged cases, leaving very few that are authentic.

Other factors that spark accusations of skepticism surround the variability in size, location, and number of wounds on stigmatics, leading some to question whether their marks are purely a psychosomatic phenomenon. Even among the holiest and most reputable stigmatics, there has been a great variety in the wounds, which understandably leads to some confusion. Photographs show that Padre Pio's wounds went through his palms, whereas Saint Francis reportedly had his stigmata through his wrists. Saint Francis's first biographer, Thomas of Celano, describes the wounds in *First Life of St. Francis* (1230):

His wrists and feet seemed to be pierced by nails, with
the heads of the nails appearing on his wrists and on
the upper sides of his feet, the points appearing on
the other side. The marks were round on the palm of
each hand but elongated on the other side, and small
pieces of flesh jutting out from the rest took on the
appearance of the nail ends, bent and driven back. In
the same way the marks of nails were impressed on his
feet and projected beyond the rest of the flesh. Moreover, his right side had a large wound as if it had been
pierced with a spear, and it often bled so that his tunic
and trousers were soaked with his sacred blood.[111]

Such a variance might suggest the possibility that the wounds
are psychologically generated in the places on the body
that the recipient associates with Christ's suffering. There
is debate about whether or not he was pierced through his
palms or his wrists. Some have suggested it is impossible to
crucify someone suspended through the palms. Nonetheless,
most artist representations show Christ hanging on the cross
through nails in his hands. Skeptics have pointed to a cor-
respondence between artwork and crucifixes owned by the
stigmatic and the marks on their bodies.[112] In other words, if
the stigmata were a real phenomenon and not influenced by
the individual's psychological state, wouldn't all stigmata be
the same (wrist wounds)? If it is true that our Lord was cru-
cified through his wrists, does this mean that stigmatics with
palm wounds do not bear the authentic wounds of Christ?

Though some speculate that the phenomenon is the result
of such psychological effects, there have been no successful
reproductions of a stigmata-like effect using the power of

suggestion in hypnosis. According to Reverend Charles M. Carty in *The Stigmata and Modern Science*, a well-regarded atheist physician from Paris, Jean-Martin Charcot (1825–1893), known as the founder of modern neurology, conducted tests on hysterical patients without any success in producing stigmata-like marks on the body. Dr. Joseph Jules Déjérine, who succeeded him, acknowledged that at his clinic there was never a single successful case of generating bleeding wounds among the large number of psychopathic patients experimented on.[113] With this being the modern scientific consensus, the hypothesis that stigmata are the result of hysteria should be safely ruled out. Yes, there are cases of fraud (self-mutilation), but it is extremely unlikely that someone could generate these physical wounds through the power of one's mind.

So what are we to conclude, then, about the stigmata? Our conclusion should be similar to many of the other miracles we have examined thus far. Yes, there are frauds and deceptions, but there are also cases where even modern science cannot offer an explanation for what is happening. In the latter cases, it is reasonable to conclude that powers beyond our earthly world have stepped in and given us a sign that there are realities we know little about at work all around us. Even so, we must not place the foundation of our faith in sensational and miraculous works. Rather, the foundation of our faith must always be rooted in Sacred Scripture and the dogmatic teachings of Holy Mother Church.

Conclusion

The conflict between faith and science has become a central element in the debate on the presence of religion in society, especially in the last fifty years. Some believers remain fearful of science, while some skeptics seem to worship science like a god. The belief in God and the denial of God's existence are two polar opposite perspectives that both require a tremendous amount of faith. (Even an atheist must place his faith in his belief of God not existing.)

Despite the Catholic Church's well-established role in the development of experimental knowledge and practice over the centuries, science is the weapon of choice for many skeptics in the dialogue with believers, harkening back to popular but settled past questions about the Catholic Church's participation in the Galileo affair, or her position on the theory of evolution. Some questions will never go away: biblical accounting for the age of the earth, the impossibility of *all* the world's land mammals fitting on Noah's ark, the apparent old age of biblical figures like Methuselah, and the lack of video evidence for modern cases of levitation (which seemed so prevalent in hagiographies of the Middle Ages), among others.

Future questions of science will always come up in the context of religion: if a human being could be cloned, would it have a soul? If intelligent non-human life were discovered, what would the Catholic Church's position be on their salvation and need for baptism? What should be done with frozen embryos?

While most all of the world's religions profess a belief in the possibility of miracles, the Catholic Church stands above the rest in its reliance on science to attempt to validate true miracles, or at least properly dismiss cases of hoaxes in order to protect the faithful in the truth. The Church stays true to its pedigree and historical connection to science by such a stringent adherence, even requiring multiple medical healings validated by a panel of doctors from various faith backgrounds in order for one of its saints to be formally recognized.

All miracles, however, are complicated in some way, leading to questions we may never have answers to. Questions like:

- Are the incorruptible bodies of saints truly miraculous when they are not perfectly preserved?
- Will we someday have an explanation for medical miracles?
- Why do the wounds of stigmatics vary from case to case?
- How do we know that Marian visionaries are telling the truth?
- When a statue weeps and there are no messages, what does it mean?
- Why do Eucharistic miracles have incomplete DNA?

With all the beauty that miracles inspire and the excitement and confidence a believer may feel from the boost of the supernatural, faith cannot be based on miracles. Likewise, even as faith is congruent with science and bolstered by science in a common pursuit of truth, faith will never need science to prove its worth. Scientific tests may never be able to prove the existence of God, but we can grow closer to God by furthering our knowledge of his creation and by marveling in the miracle of it all, especially those miracles that seem to reach beyond the limits of natural laws.

Notes

1   Interview with Fr. Paul Mueller, *The Miracle Hunter*, Relevant Radio, January 27, 2019.

2   Ibid.

3   Interview with Dr. Michael Dennin, *The Miracle Hunter*, Relevant Radio, August 8, 2016.

4   Interview with Dr. Gerard Verschuuren, *The Miracle Hunter*, Relevant Radio, October 20, 2019.

5   Interview with Fr. John Kartje, *The Miracle Hunter*, Relevant Radio, May 27, 2018.

6   Pope Francis, "Address of His Holiness Pope Francis on the Occasion of the Inauguration of the Bust in Honour of Pope Benedict XVI," October 27, 2014, http://www.vatican.va/content/francesco/en/speeches/2014/october/documents/papa-francesco_20141027_plenaria-accademia-scienze.html.

7   Joseph Ratzinger, *Salt of the Earth: The Church at the End of the Millennium-An Interview With Peter Seewald* (San Francisco: Ignatius Press, 1997).

8   Pope John Paul II, "Letter of his Holiness John Paul II to Reverend George v. Coyne, SJ, Director of the Vatican Observatory," June 1, 1988, https://www.vatican.va/content/john-paul-ii/en/letters/1988/documents/hf_jp-ii_let_19880601_padre-coyne.html.

9   *Catechism of the Catholic Church*, no. 159.

10 "About," Catholic Healthcare Association, accessed December 1, 2020, https://www.chausa.org/about/about.

11 Bruce Weber, "The Rev. Stanley L. Jaki, Physicist and Theologian Dies at 84," *The New York Times*, April 12, 2009, https://www.nytimes.com/2009/04/13/nyregion/13jaki.html.

12 Alvin J. Schmidt, *How Christianity Saved the World* (Zondervan, 2009).

13 William B. Ashworth, *God and Nature: Historical Essays on the Encounter between Christianity and Science* (Berkeley, California: University of California Press 1986), p. 154.

14   Kathleen N. Hattrup, "A thousand scientists tackle the 'science is opposed to faith' myth," *Aleteia*, May 28, 2019, https://aleteia .org/2019/05/28/scientists-explain-how-can-we-destroy-the -myth-that-faith-opposes-science/.

15   Ibid.

16   See *CCC* 548.

17   "'Virgin Mary' Underpass Stain Defaced With Devil Graffiti," Fox News, January 23, 2009, https://www.foxnews.com/story /virgin-mary-underpass-stain-defaced-with-devil-graffiti.

18   Gabrielle Calise, "Remember when the Virgin Mary appeared on a Clearwater building?" Tampa Bay Times, December 23, 2019, https://www.tampabay.com/news/florida/2019/12/23/remem ber-when-the-virgin-mary-appeared-on-a-clearwater-building/.

19   Ben Radford, *Mysterious New Mexico* (Albuquerque, NM: University of New Mexico Press, 2014), pp. 111–130.

20   https://www.catholicnewsagency.com/news/33630/italys-bleed ing-thorn-marks-the-coincidence-of-good-friday-annunciation.

21   Sperindeo Gennaro and Raffaele Januario, *Il Miracolo di S. Gennaro*, 3rd ed. (Naples: D'Auria, 1901), pp. 67–72.

22   L. Garlaschelli, F. Ramaccini, and S. Della Sala, "The Blood of St. Januarius," *Chemistry in Britain*, 30 (2):123.

23   Michael Epstein and Luigi Garlaschelli, "Better Blood Through Chemistry: A Laboratory Replication of a Miracle," *Journal of Scientific Exploration*, 6:233–246.

24   Michele De Lucia, "Miracolo di San Gennaro, un test dimostra che nell´ampolla c´è sangue umano," Naples: *Positano News*, February 2, 2010.

25   Patricia Treece, *Nothing Short of a Miracle* (Manchester, NH: Sophia Institute Press, 2013), xxix.

26   J. P. B. Goncalves, G. Luchetti, P. R. Menezes, and H. Vallada, "Religious and spiritual interventions in mental health care: a systematic review and meta-analysis of randomized controlled clinical trials," *Psychological Medicine*, July 23, 2015, https://www .ncbi.nlm.nih.gov/pmc/articles/PMC4595860/.

27   Patricia Treece, *Nothing Short of a Miracle* (Manchester, NH: Sophia Institute Press, 2013), xxix.

28   Brenda C. Coleman, "Study: Prayer Helps Heart Patients," *AP News*, October 25, 1999, https://apnews.com/article/4e 731327743c19d9a8069eabf23cdba7.

29   Jacalyn Duffin, "PRESIDENTIAL ADDRESS: The Doctor Was

Surprised; or, How to Diagnose a Miracle," *Bulletin of the History of Medicine*, Vol. 81, No. 4 (Winter 2007), pp. 699–729.

30 Joe Heschmeyer, "The Science of Miracles," *Shameless Popery* (blog), December 30, 2019, http://shamelesspopery.com/the-science-of-miracles/; Jacalyn Duffin, "PRESIDENTIAL ADDRESS: The Doctor Was Surprised; or, How to Diagnose a Miracle," https://www.jstor.org/stable/44452157.

31 Jacalyn Duffin, "PRESIDENTIAL ADDRESS: The Doctor Was Surprised; or, How to Diagnose a Miracle," pp. 699–729.

32 "How do we recognize the 70th miracle of Lourdes," Lourdes Sanctuaire, https://www.lourdes-france.org/en/how-do-we-recognise-a-lourdes-miracle/.

33 Ibid.

34 "Learn About the Waking Pill," ampyra, accessed December 1, 2020, https://ampyra.com/what-is-ampyra.

35 Patty Knap, "Arizona Woman's Blidness Miraculously Cured Through St. Charbel," *National Catholic Register*, February 15, 2017, https://www.ncregister.com/blog/arizona-womans-blindness-miraculously-cured-through-st-charbel.

36 Heather Pringle, "The Incorruptibles," *Discover*, June 2001, http://web.archive.org/web/20010610014402/http://www.discover.com/june_01/featsaints.html.

37 Joan Carroll Cruz, *The Incorruptibles: A Study of the Incorruption of the Bodies of Various Catholic Saints and Beati* (Rockford, IL:TAN Books and Publishers, 1991), p. 27.

38 Ibid., p. 31.

39 Ibid., p. 34.

40 Elizabeth Harper, "Photographing the Real Bodies of Incurrupt Saints," *Atlas Obscura*, June 30, 2015, https://www.atlasobscura.com/articles/photographing-the-real-bodies-of-incorrupt-saints.

41 Andre Ravier, "The Body of St. Bernadette of Lourdes," EWTN, https://www.ewtn.com/catholicism/library/body-of-st-bernadette-of-lourdes-5236.

42 Ibid.

43 Ibid.

44 Ibid.

45 Ibid.

46 Joan Carroll Cruz, *The Incorruptibles*, p. 40.

47 Heather Pringle, "The Incorruptibles."

48 Ibid.

49   Annetta Black, "The Incorruptible St. Zita," *Atlas Obscura*, https ://www.atlasobscura.com/places/incorruptible-st-zita.

50   "This explains the scientific testing done on 37 visionaries. The physiological changes detected in these tests could not be faked or manipulated willfully. 31 of the 37 proved to be real," *PDT signs and messages from God* (blog), http://www.pdtsigns.com/conyers .html.

51   Thea Jarvis, "NCCB Letter: Archbishop Voices Doubt On Conyers," *The Miracle Hunter* (blog), March 19, 1991, http://miraclehunter .com/marian_apparitions/statements/conyers_statement.html.

52   John Carpenter, "Science Tests the Visionaries," Divine Mysteries and Miracles (blog), May 23, 2016, http://www.divinemysteries .info/category/scientific-investigations/.

53   Ibid.

54   "Documentation," Garabandal (website), https://garabandal.it /en/documentation/statements-from-the-bishops-of-santander.

55   Ibid.

56   Doroteo, "Declaraciones Del Obispado De Santander Primera Nota Oficial De Mons. Fernandez. San Sebastian De Garabandal," The Miracle Hunter (blog), http://miraclehunter.com/marian _apparitions/statements/garabandal_19610826.html.

57   Doroteo, "Segunda Nota Oficial De Mons. Fernandez. Nota Oficial Sobre Los Sucesos De San Sebastian De Garabandal," The Miracle Hunter (blog), http://miraclehunter.com/marian _apparitions/statements/garabandal_19611101.html.

58   "Documentation," Garabandal (website), https://garabandal.it/en /documentation/statements-from-the-bishops-of-santander.

59   Ibid.

60   Donal Anthony Foley, *Medjugorje Revisited: 30 Years of Visions or Religious Fraud?* (Nottingham, England: Theotokos Books, 2011).

61   John Carpenter, "Science Tests the Visionaries," Divine Mysteries and Miracles (blog), May 23, 2016, http://www.divinemysteries .info/science-tests-the-visionaries/.

62   Ibid.

63   Ibid.

64   T. Kammerer, Critical Study of Medical Explorations of the Medjugorje Seers, LIMC, 20 September 1986, https://en.marco corvaglia.com/uno-studio-critico-del-prof-kammere.

65   Marco Corvaglia, "Medical Tests on the Seers: Science Demon- strates Nothing," The Medjugorje Illusion (blog), July 10, 2009,

https://en.marcocorvaglia.com/la-scienza-non-prova-nulla-parte-1.

66   Ibid.

67   James Mulligan, *Medjugorje: The First Days* (CreateSpace, 2013), p. 193.

68   "Medjugorje Commission: Leaked Final Report," Kevin J. Symonds (blog), February 20, 2020, https://kevinsymonds.com /2020/02/20/medjugorje-leaked-report/.

69   Just before this book went to press, Archbishop Hoser died on August 13, 2021.

70   *Compendium of the Catechism of the Catholic Church*, no. 274, http://www.vatican.va/archive/compendium_ccc/documents /archive_2005_compendium-ccc_en.html.

71   "The Eucharistic Miracles of the World Exhibition," Real Presence Eucharistic Education and Adoration Association, accessed January 1, 2021, http://therealpresence.org/eucharst/mir/engl_mir.htm.

72   Ibid.

73   Albert Vogl, *Life and Death of Therese Neumann, Mystic and Stigmatist* (New York, NY:Vantage Press, 1978), p. 2.

74   "Utah diocese: Miracles happen. The 'bleeding' Host wasn't one," *Catholic News Agency*, December 17, 2015, https://www.catholic newsagency.com/news/33173/utah-diocese-miracles-happen-the -bleeding-host-wasnt-one.

75   Ashton Edwards, "'Bleeding host' was mold, not miracle, according to diocese," Fox 13, December 16, 2015, https://www.fox13now .com/2015/12/16/bleeding-host-was-mold-not-miracle-according -to-diocese/.

76   "Eucharistic Miracle," Reason to Believe (blog), https://reason tobelieve.com.au/eucharistic-miracle/.

77   "The Eucharistic Miracles of Buenos Aires," Edizioni San Clemente, 2006, http://www.therealpresence.org/eucharst/mir/english _pdf/BuenosAires3.pdf.

78   Eucharistic Miracle," Reason to Believe (blog), https://reasontobe lieve.com.au/eucharistic-miracle/.

79   "Eucharistic Miracle of Tixtla," Edizioni San Clemente, 2006, http://www.therealpresence.org/eucharst/mir/english_pdf/Tixt la2.pdf.

80   Philip Kosloski, "How a Eucharistic miracle is approved by the Church," *Aleteia*, June 1, 2018, https://aleteia.org/2018/06/01 /how-a-eucharistic-miracle-is-approved-by-the-church/.

81   Interview with Fr. Robert Spitzer, "The Miracle Hunt-

er," EWTN Radio, June 26, 2021, https://listen.ewtn.com/~OM/~OM20210612.mp3.

82 "The Eucharistic miracle of Sokolka: The host is tissue from heart of a dying man," *Aleteia*, September 23, 2017, https://aleteia.org/2017/09/23/the-eucharistic-miracle-of-sokolka-the-host-is-tissue-from-heart-of-a-dying-man/.

83 "Wow Eucharistic #Miracle in Poland approved by Bishop proven by DNA testing – SHARE," Catholic News World (blog), April 17, 2016, http://www.catholicnewsworld.com/2016/04/wow-eucharistic-miracle-in-poland.html.

84 "Pastoral Letter of Bishop John Shojiro Ito April 22, 1984," The Miracle Hunter (blog), http://www.miraclehunter.com/marian_apparitions/statements/akita_statement_01.html; Francis Mutsuo Fukushima, *Akita: Mother of God as CoRedemptrix* (Modern Miracles of Holy Eucharist, Publishing Company, 1997).

85 John Ata, "A Message From Our Lady – Akita, Japan," November 2011, https://www.ewtn.com/catholicism/library/message-from-our-lady--akita-japan-5167.

86 Stefano M. Paci, "The Tears of Akita," *30 Days*, July–August 1990, 45.

87 Jim Carney, *The Seton Miracles: Weeping Statues and Other Wonders* (Marian Foundation, 1998).

88 Stephen Ryan, "Pedophile Priest Who Commited Suicide Was Central Figure in Shutting Down The Greatest Manifestation of Weeping Statues in the History of the World that Haunted Justice Scalia Until He Died," *Mystic Post*, August 14, 2018, https://mysticpost.com/2018/08/the-extraordinary-case-of-weeping-statues-of-the-virgin-mary-in-washington-dc-and-the-clerical-sex-abuse-crisis-our-ladys-tears-go-unanswered-justice-scalia-beleived/.

89 "'We Have Not Discerned Natural Causes': Bishop Issues Incredible Report on Crying Statue Miracle," *ChurchPOP*, September 8, 2018, https://www.churchpop.com/2018/09/08/we-have-not-discerned-natural-causes-bishop-issues-incredible-report-on-crying-statue/.

90 Philippe Loron, "Constat Médical et Analyses Scientifiques Des Événements de SOUFANIEH - 12 - 16 avril 1990," (Paris: Éditions F. X. de Guibert), http://web.archive.org/web/20170723094653/https://www.soufanieh.com/MEDICAL/HUILE/19900416.fra.eng.chromatography.oil.htm.

91 Ibid.

[92] "The Oil," https://www.soufanieh.com/ENGLISH/oil.htm.

[93] "The Weeping Madonna of Syracuse," http://www.catholic tradition.org/Mary/syracuse.htm.

[94] Ibid.

[95] "Church Approved Weeping Events," The Marian Foundation, http://www.thesetonmiracles.org/other-weeping-events.

[96] "The Weeping Madonna of Syracuse," http://www.catholic tradition.org/Mary/syracuse.htm.

[97] "Church Approved Weeping Events," The Marian Foundation, http://www.thesetonmiracles.org/other-weeping-events.

[98] G. K. Chesterton, *St. Francis of Assisi* (Garden City, New York: Image Books, 1924), p. 131.

[99] Mike Dash, "The Mystery of the Five Wounds," *Smithsonian Magazine*, November 18, 2011, http://www.smithsonianmag.com/history/the-mystery-of-the-five-wounds-361799.

[100] René Biot, *The Enigma of the Stigmata* (New York: Hawthorn Books, 1962), p. 20.

[101] Joe Nickell, *The Science of Miracles* (New York: Prometheus Books, 2013), p. 324.

[102] Michael P. Carroll, *Catholic Cults and Devotions: A Psychological Inquiry* (Montreal: McGill University Press, 1989), pp. 80–84.

[103] "Details of first investigation into Padre Pio's stigmata revealed," *Catholic News Agency*, September 22, 2008, https://www.catholic newsagency.com/news/13863/details-of-first-investigation-into -padre-pios-stigmata-revealed.

[104] Bernard Ruffin, *Padre Pio: The True Story* (Huntington, IN: Our Sunday Visitor, 1991), pp. 160–163.

[105] Malcolm Moore, "Italy's Padre Pio 'Faked His Stigmata with Acid,'" *Daily Telegraph*, October 24, 2007.

[106] Lawrence Segel, "The inexplicable phenomenon of the Stigmata," accessed November 30, 2021, https://www.soufanieh.com/MED ICAL/19970806.CAN.ENG.DR.SEGEL.LAWRENCE.pdf.

[107] Ibid.

[108] Ibid.

[109] Brigid Keenan, "Myrna and the Oil an Everyday Miracle: How Does a Woman Become a Modern Saint? In Damascus Brigid Keenna Met Myrna Nazzour and Saw for Herself . . .' *Independent*, August 10, 1994, https://www.independent.co.uk /life-style/myrna-and-the-oil-an-everyday-miracle-how-does-a -woman-become-a-modern-saint-in-damascus-brigid-keenan

-met-myrna-nazzour-and-saw-for-herself-1375732.html.

110 sd, "Pope To Visit Mosul Churches," *Spirit Daily* (blog), March 2, 2021, https://spiritdailyblog.com/news/pope-to-visit-mosul-churches.

111 Paul Halsall, *Medieval Sourcebook: Thomas of Celano: First and Second Lives of St. Francis*, trans. David Burr (Fordham University, 1996), http://legacy.fordham.edu/halsall/ source/stfran-lives.html.

112 Ted Harrison, *Stigmata: A Medieval Phenomenon in a Modern Age* (New York: St. Martin's Press, 1994), p. 128.

113 Joe Nickell, *The Mystery Chronicles: More Real-Life X-Files* (Lexington, KY: University Press of Kentucky, 2004), p. 242.